1 MONTH OF
FREE
READING

at
www.ForgottenBooks.com

By purchasing this book you are
eligible for one month membership to
ForgottenBooks.com, giving you
unlimited access to our entire
collection of over 1,000,000 titles via
our web site and mobile apps.

To claim your free month visit:
www.forgottenbooks.com/free1236366

ISBN 978-0-332-73844-4
PIBN 11236366

Foreword

To you, the students and all who know Decatur High School life, this book is presented with the desire that in it you may find reflections of happiness; reflections of pleasant memories and inspirations; reflections of beauty that will make life worth the living and a more determined, "We can because we think we can."

We hope that on each page you may find some expression of school life which has been both joyful and valuable.

To

Mrs. Minnie P. Hostetler

· Dean of Girls
Instructor of Mathematics

A Wise and Understanding Instructor
Who has Consistently Stood for all
That is Best in Life

We

The Class of Nineteen twenty-three

Dedicate

This Tenth Volume of the
Decanois

Decanois Staff

Editor-in-Chief ....W. JUNIOR ROTHFUSS
Business Manager ....JAMES RATTAN
Advertising Manager ....WILLIAM PITNER
Assistant Editor-in-Chief ....BONNIE REGAN
Assistant Business Manager ....ROGER YODER
Assistant Advertising Manager ....JOSEPH ROSENBERG
Quotation Editors ....LOUISE DENZ, ESTHER BARNETT
Literary Editor ....HERMAN PRITCHETT
Societies Editor ....LEALDES EATON
Local Editors ....EVERETT WITZEMAN, FANNY POWERS
Calendar Editors .....VIRGINIA DAWSON, VIRGINIA HOLMES
Joke Editors ....BETTIE HOLT, JACK HENDERSON
Snapshot Editor ....ROLLIN PEASE
Athletic Editors ....HELEN HAYS, GLENN McCLELLAND
Stenographer ....NELLIE WEBER

THE DECANOIS STAFF 1923

Editor in Chief   Business Manager   Advertising Manager   Quotation Editor

Assistant Editor   Asst Business Mgr   Asst. Adv. Manager   Quotation Editor

Literary Editor   Societies Editor   Locals Editor   Locals Editor

Calendar Editor   Calendar Editor   Athletics Editor   Athletics Editor

Jokes Editor   Jokes Editor   Snapshots Editor   Stenographer

Decanois Art Staff

Editor-in-chief

HELEN E. HACKETT

Assistant Editors

ESTHER SCRANTON	JANICE WIDICK
ANNA WALKER	CLAIRBELLE FISK
LESTER FOLTZ	ALICE COLVIN, '24
RUSSELL SIX	CATHERINE SCURLOCK, '24
FRANCES SELLARS	ROLAND TAYLOR, '25
LUCILLE CHRONISTER	JEANETTE POWELL, '24

Cartoonists

WALLACE HOGLE　　　　TOM RIGGS, '24

ROLANDA BROSSEAU, '24

THE DECANOIS ART STAFF

Ode to the Faculty

Yes, indeed, we are the Seniors of the Class of Twenty-three.
Don't you think this gives me joy?   Oh, it's happiness to me.
Though some have toiled and studied and some have tried to shirk.
We're indebted to the teachers, who tried to make us work.

Though some have used their ponies and bluffed through day by day,
They'll find that in the long run it didn't really pay.
And when they battle with the world and troubles 'round them lurk,
They'll think often of the teachers who tried to make them work.

And those who've studied faithfully, and worked before they'd play,
Will some day be rewarded, though how, we cannot say.
But no matter where they labor, or where they cross the river,
They'll think of the teachers kind who wear the Blue and Silver.

And so, you see, the teachers are the ones we ought to praise,
For they've endured our dumbness through many weary days,
And have led us on to glory.   Well, yes, I guess!
So here's to the teachers of our dear old D. H. S.

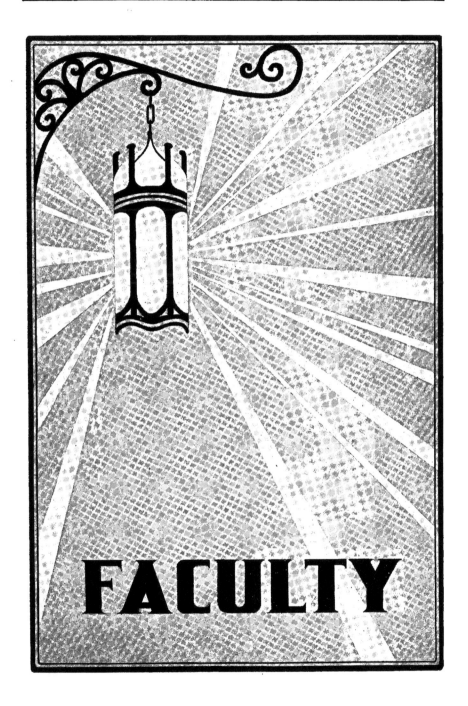

FACULTY

MR. THOMAS M. DEAM, A. B., A. M.
·September, 1913
University of Indiana, Columbia University, University of Chicago.
Principal of High School, Sociology.

MISS OLIVE M. BEAR, M. L.
September, 1899
Knox College, Cornell, University of Chicago.
Head of English department, Senior Advisor, Observer Advisor.

MR. ASA SPRUNGER, A. B.
September, 1916
Oberlin College.
Assistant Principal, Dean of Boys, Botany, Zoology.

MRS. LUCY H. NELSON
September, 1912
Columbia University, University of Chicago.
English, Junior Advisor, Agora Advisor.

MRS. MINNIE P. HOSTETLER, A. B.
September, 1882
University of Illinois.
Dean of Girls, Geometry, Algebra.

MISS ELIZA THOMAS, A. B.
September, 1914
Boston University, University of Chicago.
English, Dramatic Coach, Mask and Wig Advisor.

MISS MARY L. ENGLISH
March, 1901
Columbia University, Leland Stanford University, University of Chicago.
Head of Latin Department, Chairman of Senior Advisors.

MISS LOIS YODER, A. B.
September, 1918
Millikin University.
English, Aristos Advisor.

MRS. ERNA R. OWENS, A. B.	MISS CORINNE PENROD, A. B.
September, 1919	September, 1920
University of Illinois.	University of Indiana.
English, Sophomore Advisor.	English.

MISS ESTELLE FRITTER, B. Ed.	MISS NELLE F. BARTELS, A. B.
September, 1919	September 1921
I. S. N. U., Columbia University, University of Middle Tennessee.	University of Illinois, Columbia University.
English, Senior Advisor, Decanois Advisor.	English.

MISS CLEDA V. MOSES, A. B.	MISS ZUA SHOEMAKER, B. S., A. B.
February, 1920	February, 1922
University of Illinois, I. S. N. U., Smith College.	University of Ohio.
English.	English.

MISS GRACE JACKSON, A. B.	MISS CLARA J. HADLEY
September 1919	September, 1920
University of Indiana, University of Chicago, Columbia University.	Butler College, Earlham, Indiana State Normal.
English.	Librarian.

MISS MARY CARROLL, A. B.

September, 1914

Millikin University, University of Illinois.
Latin, Spanish.

MISS MARY LILLIAN CREA, A. B.

February, 1919

Vassar, University of Chicago, Madrid
(Spain) University.
Head of Spanish department.

MISS MARY McINTIRE, A. B.

September, 1919

University of Illinois.
Latin.

MISS LIDA C. MARTIN, B. L.

September, 1900

University of Michigan, N. I. S. N. S.
Head of the Mathematics department.

MISS RUBY ENGLE, A. B.

September, 1919

University of Indiana.
Latin.

MISS INEZ WHITCRAFT, A. B., A. M.

September, 1920

Indiana State Normal, University of Indiana.
Geometry, Algebra.

MISS ESTHER KINSEY, A. B.

September, 1920

University of Illinois.
Head of French department.

MISS LUCY DURFEE, A. B., A. M.

September, 1904

Michigan University, Columbia University.
University of Chicago.
Algebra, Geometry.

MISS LOIS ROBERTS, A. B.

September, 1922

I. S. N. U., Millikin, University of Illinois,
University of Chicago.
Geometry.

MISS ELLEN HENNINGER, A. B.

September, 1919

Illinois Wesleyan, I. S. N. U., University
of Chicago.
Modern History.

MISS RUTH GRANT, A. B.

November, 1922

University of Illinois.
Algebra, Geometry.

MR. O. S. HUBBART, A. B., A. M.

September, 1920

Northwestern University, University of
Illinois.
Economics, Civics, Forum Advisor.

MISS GRACE BRIDGES, Ph. B.

September, 1918

Kirkville State Normal, University of Chicago.
Head of History department, Senior Advisor.

MR. B. F. NORDMAN, A B., A. M.

September, 1920

Leland Stanford University.
Modern History, Rotaro Adviser.

MISS ANNA HULL, A. B., A. M.

September, 1918

University of Illinois.
Modern History, English History, Head of
Junior Advisor.

MISS GERTRUDE HILL, A. B.

September, 1920

Eastern Illinois Normal, University of Illinois, University of Chicago.
American History.

MISS MOLLIE DROBISCH, A. B.

January, 1921

University of Illinois, University of Chicago, Columbia University.
Early European History, Modern History.

MISS MARY EARNEST

February, 1918

Indiana State Normal, University of Chicago. .
Botany, Zoology.

MISS BLANCHE CHEVILLION, B. S.

September, 1919

Carthage College, University of Chicago.
Early European History.

MISS MAE ORMSBY, A. B.

September, 1919

University of Illinois, University of Chicago.
Physiology, Junior Advisor.

MR. E. H. WESTLUND, B. S., Ph. C.

September, 1918

Purdue University, University of Illinois.
Head of Chemistry department, Basketball Manager, Advisor to Science Club.

MR. DONALD B. MILLER, A. B.

September, 1921

University of Iowa.
Chemistry.

MR. H. H. RADCLIFFE, A. B.

September, 1918

University of Indiana, University of Wisconsin, Indiana State Normal, University of Illinois.
Head of Physics department, Senior Advisor.

MR. A. C. HAMMOND

September, 1922

University of Illinois.
Head of Agriculture Department. Advisor of Agriculture Club.

MR. WILLIAM HEINLE, B. Acc't.

April, 1918

Valparaiso University.
Bookkeeping, Band Advisor.

MISS HALLIE. MILLER

September, 1918

Millikin University.
Com. Arithmetic.

MISS MARY PARKER, A. B., B. Pd.

September, 1912

Michigan Normal, University of Michigan.
Needham Business College, Gregg School
Stenography.

MISS NAOMA ENGLE

September, 1920

Indiana Normal, Gregg School, Wisconsin
State Normal.
Typewriting.

MISS WINNIFRED WILSON, A. B.

February, 1914

University of Michigan.
Bookkeeping, Stenography, High School
Auditor.

MR. JAMES G. ALLEN, LI. B.

February, 1923

Kansas State Normal, Northwestern University.
Com. Arithmetic, Com. Law, Bookkeeping.

MISS ONA GIFFIN, B. S.

February, 1917

Valparaiso University, University of Illinois.
Bookkeeping. Com. Arithmetic, Com. Ge-
ography, Business English.

MRS. MAUDE C. MEYER, B. S.

September, 1920

Millikin University, Applied Arts School of
Chicago.
Head of Art Department, Advisor to Art
Clubs.

MISS HELEN MURPHY, B. S. September, 1913 Columbia University, Michigan State Normal. Head of Domestic Science Department.	MR. V. J. RICE, B. S. September, 1920 Indiana Normal. Joinery, Cabinet Making, Woodworking.
MISS KATHERINE TROUTMAN, A. B. September, 1917 Millikin University, Wisconsin University, Columbia University. Domestic Science.	MR. LAWRENCE ROTZ November, 1919 Millikin University, Bradley Polytechnic Institute. Mechanical Drawing.
MISS EFFIE THEOBALD, B. S. September, 1920 Women's College, Columbia University: Domestic Art.	MR. FREDERICK SCHMIDT September, 1921 Professional Training. Forge.
MR. HENRY A. BOHL September, 1922 University of Michigan, Millikin University. Manual Training Department.	MR. WILLIAM MUIR, B. S. September, 1920 University of Missouri, University of Illinois. Head of Boys' Physical Education Department, Athletic Coach.

MRS. MARION LYCAN, B. S.

September, 1921

University of Ohio, Sargent School for Physical Education.
Head of Girls' Physical Education Department.

MR. JOSEPH TOMMASI, B. M. A.

October, 1922

University of Naples, Naples Royal Conservatory of Music.
Head of Music Department, Advisor to Musical Clubs.

MISS VEDA WALKER

September, 1920

Brown's Business College.
Secretary to Principal.

MISS ELSIE PARKER

November, 1920

Decatur High School.
Assistant Secretary to Principal.

We Can Because
We Think We Can
—The Senior Class

Committees of Senior Class

Ring and Pin

James Rattan (Chairman)
Tom Bohon
Bonnie Regan

Athletic

Howard Kile (Chairman)
Paul Lewis
Helen Hays
Cora Michener

Constitutional

Lester Foltz (Chairman)
Lealdes Eaton
Bettie Holt
Virginia Dawson
Bonnie Regan

Floral

Bettie Holt (Chairman)
Lealdes Eaton
Esther Scranton

Color

James Rattan (Chairman)
Junior Rothfuss
Dorothy Wilson
Bonnie Regan

Play

Ermina Busch (Chairman)
Helen Krumsiek
Richard Golden

Motto

Everett Witzeman (Chairman)
Lester Foltz
Louise Denz
Clairbelle Fisk

Class Day Program

Tom Bohon (Chairman)
Junior Rothfuss
Margaret Humphrey
Eugene Danzeisen
Cora Michener

Social

Dorothy Wilson (Chairman)
Everett Witzeman
Louise Denz
Junior Rothfuss
Imelda Curran
Russell Six
Iva Brennen
Lester Foltz
Lealdes Eaton
Esther Scranton

Commencement Program

Lealdes Eaton (Chairman)
Ermina Busch
William Pitner
Constance Waltz
Everett Witzeman

Class Officers

President—GLENN McCLELLAND

A man, Roman from head to heel, and Roman of the noblest.

Rotaro, '20, '21; Pub. Spkg, Board of Control, '22, '23; Hi-Y, '19, '20, '21, '22 '23; (Pres. '22); Silver Delta, '21; Football, '22; Charleston Oratorical Contest, '22; "Such a Little Queen"; Decanois Staff, '23; Valedictorian.

Vice-President—DOROTHY E. WILSON

She has the triune of perfect starriness which makes all men astronomers.

Agora, '22, '23; Arion, '20, '21; Jr. Art League, '20; Social Science Club, '22; Tri-Y, '22, '23; "Such a Little Queen".

Secretary—BONNIE R. REGAN

Such a little queen!

Arion, '21, 22; Agora, '21, '22, '23; Mask and Wig, '20, '21, '22, '23; Silver Delta, '21; Decanois Staff, '23; "Such a Little Queen".

Treasurer—W. JUNIOR ROTHFUSS

Splendid as a general's plume at full gallop.

Rotaro, '19, '20, '21, '22, '23; (Pres. '22); Science Club, '22; Social Science Club, '22; Class Baseball, '20; Silver Delta, '21; Hi-Y, '23; Decanois Staff, '22, '23.

MURRIEL ABELL

I think content is a luxury.
Arion, '20, '21; Agora, '22, '23; Commercial
Club, '23; G. A. A., '20, '21; Science Club,
'22.

RUTH ACKERMAN

I am splendid, thanks.
Arion, '21; Aristos, '22, '23; Mask & Wig,
'22, '23; Observer Staff, '22, '23; "Tailor
Made Man"; "'Op o' Me Thumb"; "The
Turtle Dove".

ANNIE LUCILLE ADAMS

*The world has faults; mountains have
chasms, but to me the effect of the whole
is sublime.*
Arion, '21, '22; Agora, '22, 23; G. A. A. '22,
'23; Mask & Wig, '21, '22, '23; Poster Club,
'21.

ETHEL G. ADAMS

*I can bear the examinations of sober
thought.*
Commercial Club, '22, '23; Science Club,
'22; Girls' Glee Club, '22, '23.

HOWARD F. ADKINS

Studies, I think, are rather a thin cracker.
Football, 21, '22.

HELEN MADGE ALBERT

*I shall carry my pitcher of curiosity to an-
other fountain.*

GRACE M. ANDERSON

*Each of those spreading maples is a friend
to me.*
Aristos, '22, '23.

MERLE ASHE

She has the tempting gift of silence.

HERBERT AUSTIN

The lines of his character are few.

Forum, '21, '22, '23; Class Basketball, '21; Football, '22.

RAY BAILEY

His look has a cumulative quality.

VIRGIL BAILEY

Ruled by a majestic doubt.

Hi-Y, '21, '22.

CHARLES C. BARNARD

Women swim in infidelity, from wave to wave—I know them.

Mask & Wig, '22, '23; Hi-Y, '22, '23; "Two Crooks and a Lady"; "Man Who Married a Dumb Wife"; "Such a Little Queen".

ESTHER BARNETT

An outburst of silence.

Aristos, '21, '22, '23; Mask & Wig, '22, '23; Decanois Staff, '23.

DOROTHY BARNHART

Eyes steady with thoughtfulness.

Arion, '19, '20; Aristos. '21, '22; Oikos, '20, '21; Orpheus, '19, '20, '21.

ANNA MAY BAUER

Not addicted to surprises.

Commercial Club, '23.

BERNICE BECKOLD

She has the glory of the racing cutter, full sail on a winning breeze.

Arion, '21; Agora, '22, '23; Ethical Club, '22, '23; Mask & Wig, '22, '23; Social Science Club, '22, '23; G. A. A., '21, '22, '23; Basketball, '21; Track, '21; "The Man Who Married a Dumb Wife".

BERNICE BELDEN
Where vigor and gentleness meet.
Arion, '20·

BERNARD BLAZER
The letter I is a soldierly letter.

MABEL MARGUERITTE BLEDSOE
Je suis contente.
Aristos, '22; Jr. Art League, '22; Poster
Club, '22·

TOM K. BOHON
When the lady died, he fell on his sword.
Boys' Glee Club, '20; Forum, '20· '21; Mask
& Wig, '22; Rotaro, '22; "No Smoking".

VELMA BONE
I look with interest into the world's mirror.
Aristos, '21· '22· '23; Ethical Club, '22· '23;
Social Science Club, '23·

ROY M. BRADY
I judge by character.
Rotaro, '21; Observer Staff, '22· '23; Hi-Y,
'22· '23; "Such a Little Queen".

FOSTER H. BRASHEAR
There's nothing of the rogue in him.
Boys' Glee Club, '21· '22· '23·

IVA BRENNEN
*Give me a rain-check for that wonderful
time.*

HELEN BRICKER
A sureness in the carriage of her head.

TED BROWN
You can't say what you mean in English.
"Ag" Club, '21' '22' '23; Boys' Glee Club,
'20, '21, '22' (Pres.) '23; Class Basketball,
'20'

MINNIE BRUBECK
I am stabbed with laughter.
Girl's Glee Club, '22' '23'

MABLE LETITIA BRUNDAGE
I am not naturalized in the world of grief.

MIRIAM MARTHA BRUNER
She has lips that smile in repose.
Aristos, '22, '23; Commercial Club, '23;
Ethical Club, '23'

EVELYN ESTELLE BURCHAM
I am bound up in a good opinion of you.

J. EMERSON BURCHELL
I would not smash my goods to kill a rat.
Rotaro, '21' '22; Football, '21'

MILDRED BURKE
Eighteen and perfect manners.

RUTH BURNETTE
I am robbed of my treasure—delusion.
Commercial Club, '22, '23.

ERMINA BUSCH
Gifted with a certain inscrutableness.
Arion, '20; Agora, '21, '22, '23; Mask &
Wig, '21, '22, '23; Class Basketball, '23;
G. A. A., '23; Tri-Y, '23; "The Seven Keys
to Baldpate"; "The Tailor Made Man";
"The Man Who Married the Dumb Wife";
"Such a Little Queen".

MARY ELIZABETH CASNER
A sunny, Epicurean smile.

LUCILLE G. CHAILLE
Alive and quick in the soul.
Agora, '23; Mask & Wig, '21, '22, '23; So-
cial Science Club, '22, '23.

ALAN CHAPMAN
*He talks as one exalting on the mountain
top.*
Forum, '22, '23; Science Club, '22, '23.

SYBIL BERNICE CHISM
Pathos is not the cargo of my ship.
Jr. Art League, '22; Poster Club, '22.

LUCILLE CHRONISTER
Life has never shaken her at all.
Jr. Art League, '22; Poster Club, '22.

HENRIETTA CLARK
*A feminine shuttle of decision is at work
in her head.*
Orchestra, '22, '23.

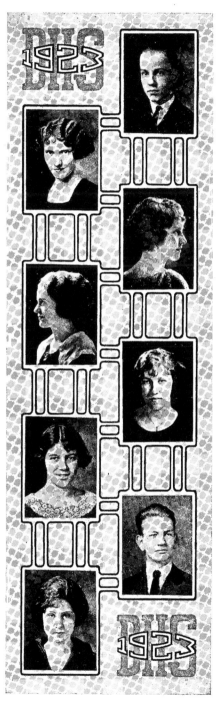

THOMAS S. CLARK

Adust and athirst for the winning post.

Rotaro, '22, '23; Debate, '23.

HELEN B. CLAYTON

The superlative is magnetic to her.

Arion, '21, '22; Agora, '22, '23; Science Club, '22, '23; Class Basketball, '22, '23; Hockey, '22; G. A. A., '20, '21, '22, '23; Tri-Y, '22, '23; House of Representatives, '21; Girls' Glee Club, '22, '23.

HELEN CLEMENTS

The will is the thing.

Social Science Club, '22, '23; Class Basketball, '23; Hockey, '23; G. A. A., '22, '23.

LOCKIE VORIS CLINE

Hew to the line, let the quips fall as they may.

Aristos, '22, '23; Ethical Club, '22, '23.

JENNIE COCHRAN

I believe I am dead and buried and that this old place is heaven.

Commercial Club, '23; Tri-Y, '23; G. A. A., '22, '23; "Feast of the Little Lantern".

FLORENCE B. COLES

In women, distinction is the thing to be aimed at.

Arion, '20, '21; Agora, '22, '23; Mask & Wig, '22, '23; Social Science Club, '22, '23; Observer Staff, '23; Hockey, '21; G. A. A., '21; "Spreading the News".

MONTFORD COLLINS

Orthodox and dignified.

"Such a Little Queen".

ELOISE CONATY

Depressed? No. I have no cause to be.

Arion, '20, '21; Girls' Class Basketball, '21, '22, '23; Girls' Class Baseball, '21, '22, '23; Hockey, '21, '22, '23; G. A. A., '21, '22, '23; Girls' Glee Club, '22, '23.

MARY CONOVER
She is made for light occasions.

ALBERTA CONSTANT
Her features are play-fellows.
Commercial Club, '22, '23.

THELMA COPE
There is a stillness that marks her personality.

TED CORRINGTON
There seemed a heart to his gravity.

RUTH CRATZ
A quiet dignity.

WALTER EDISON CUNNINGHAM
A man hard to deceive.
Boys' Glee Club, '22, '23; Forum, '23; Social Science Club, '23.

IMELDA J. CURRAN
There is a driving force in her personality.

EUGENE B. DANZEISEN
It's on the up grade, but I'm going.
Mask & Wig, '21, '22, '23; Pub. Spkg. Brd. of Control, '22, '23; Rotaro, '21, '22, '23; Observer Staff, '22, '23; "Tailor Made Man"; "Man That Married a Dumb Wife"; "Such a Little Queen"; "Spreading the News".

DOROTHY DEAN DAVIDSON
Sweet as the dew on the jasmine.
Arion, '21; Aristos, '22, '23; Library Club,
'21.

HERBERT DAVIS
Oh, the wonder and the weight of life!
"Ag" Club, '21, '22; Class Basketball, '20;
Football, '20, '21; Class Baseball, '21.

VIRGINIA DAWSON
She has a pale, wind-sheltered loveliness.
Arion, '20; Decanois Staff.

MERRILL W. DeBAUM
I'd like a cruise into the unknown.
Class Baseball, '22, '22; Commencement
Program.

LOUISE ELISABETH DENZ
Notice the adaptable people; they are invariably the interesting, attractive and lovable people.
Arion, '19, '20; Aristos, '22, '23; House of
Representatives, '19, '20; Decanois Staff,
'23.

LEE GERALD DICKINSON
He shows the cleanest candor.
Forum, '22, '23.

ELEANORA DITTUS
An unbreakable spirit; she seems to mind nothing in the world.
Ethical Club, '22, '23.

NELLIE E. DONEY
Why is it that in this world realization is so difficult a thing?

DOROTHY DRENNAN

Her look is at the same time confident and critical.

Arion, '20, '21; Agora, '21, '22, '23; Orpheus '21, '22; Observer Staff, '21; Review Story Contest, '20.

IRMA DUNN

Let nothing you dismay.

Aristos, '22, '23.

ERNEST EARLE

That's not in my character. I'd never do harm to any one.

Mask & Wig, '22, '23; "The Man Who Married a Dumb Wife".

GUYNETH EATON

Circumstances have not dimmed me.

Science Club, '22; G. A. A., '22.

LEALDES EATON

I am lying dead and cold somewhere in the corner of her heart.

Band, '21, '22; Orchestra, '20, '21; Rotaro, '21, '22; Science Club, '21, (Pres) '22; Hi-Y, '21, '22, (Pres.), '23; Decanois Staff.

ESTHER EBERT

Cool and deliberate in thought.

MATHIAS FRANKLIN ECKERT

He has a modern sense of expediency.

"Ag" Club, '21, '22 (Pres.), '23 (Pres.); Forum, '22, '23; Boys' Glee Club, '21, '22, '23.

JOHN MARION ECKMAN

He has marketable talents.

"Seven Keys to Baldpate"; Senior Play of '21; "The Tailor Made Man"; Senior Play of '22; "The Man Who Married the Dumb Wife"; "Such a Little Queen".

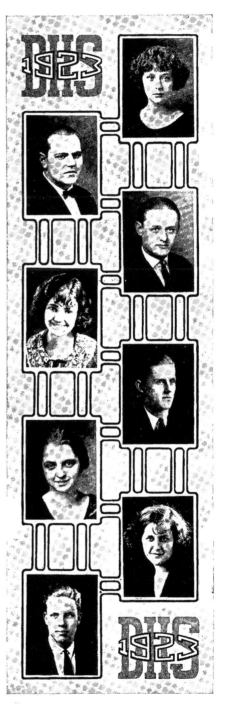

LUCILLE EHRHART

To pique, to puzzle and to please.

Hockey, '19, '21, '22; G. A. A., '19, '21, '22.

JACK A. EISELE

I'm not a man, but a mob.

"Ag" Club, '20; Forum, '23.

LOREN E. ELROD

Just like Alladin, I was picked up and set down with a boom.

FLORENCE EMME

A shy, unwilling sweetness.

Orchestra, '21.

FRANK C. ENGLISH

Eyes like an unsheathed sword.

Rotaro, '20, '21, '22, '23; Science Club, '22, '23; Hi-Y, '22, '23.

MAURINE L. EVANS

These are magic moments that peep through the grey of hard work.

Arion, '20, '21; Mask & Wig, '21, '22, '23; Review Story Contest, '22; "Two Crooks and a Lady".

CLAIRBELLE FISK

I should love to have a maid at my trunks.

Jr. Art League, '22, '23; G. A. A., '21; Poster Club, '22, '23; Pres. of Jr. Art League, '22.

LESTER H. FOLTZ

Nothing, I think, is more conspicuous than melancholy.

Class Basketball, '21, '22, '23; Jr. Art League, '22; Poster Club, '22, '23; Student Council; Observer Staff; Decanois Staff; "Such a Little Queen".

EUGENE FRANCIS FORAN

An old-fashioned standard of good faith.

Boys' Glee Club, '22, '23; Commercial Club, '23; Class Basketball, '22, '23; Class Baseball, '20, '21.

HARRIET A. FOULKE

I like people to be cheerful and witty.

Aristos, '22, '23; Ethical Club, '23; Social Science Club, '22, '23.

CHARLES FRAZIER

I believe that frivolity is a quality that belongs in the same box with the powder puff.

FERNE M. GARMAN

She liked people to be sure of themselves.

Ethical Club, '22, '23.

MERTON GARVER

The eye of watch-maker.

"Ag" Club, '21, '22, '23.

CARRIE ELLEN GASAWAY

My happiness is acute.

JESSIE GLASGOW

She can stand anything without getting sour or small.

Ethical Club, '22, '23; Oikos, '22; Poster Club, '22, '23; Debating, '22.

HAROLD C. GLATZ

He has no time for sky-larking.

RICHARD GOLDEN
He does not discuss his ambitions.

CARL GOODWIN
He'll be a substantial prop for the American Nation.
Commercial Club, '22, '23 (pres.); Rotaro, '21, '22, '23; Class Basketball, '20, '22; Hi-Y, '23; Observer Staff, '22, '23.

CATHERINE GRAHAM
She loves sport, the exciting kind.
Arion, '21; Agora, '22, '23; Oikos, '22; Social Science Club, '22; Girls' Class Baseball, '21, '22, '23; Track, '21; Hockey, '21, '23; G. A. A., '21, '22, '23; Baseball, '20, '21, '22, '23; Volley Ball, '23.

VIRGINIA GRAY
A person of birth.
Arion, '20.

RUTH M. GROTHE
Happiness is not the result of events, but of character.
Ethical Club, '22, '23.

AUDREY GRUBB
The heat of the day means nothing to her.

EVELYN CORINNE GULICK
A nine days' wonder.
Jr. Art League, '22.

HELEN E. HACKETT
Teeming with talent.
Jr. Art League, '23; Poster Club, '23.

DOROTHY A. HAMBRIGHT

Yes, the world is good after all, very good.

Arion, '19, '20; Agora, '21, '22, '23; Observer Staff, '20; Hockey, '20, '21, '22; G. A. A., '19, '20, '21, '22.

WILLARD S. HANSEN

He is good deal of a man.

Forum, '21, '22, '23; Science Club, '23; Pres. of Forum, '23; "Trial By Jury".

LESLIE HARKNESS

He furnishes excitement free of charge.

Band, '21, '22, '23; Orchestra, '20, '21, '22, '23; Orpheus, '20, '21.

JAMES HARMON

He is a good fellow, unpretentious and kindly.

HELEN MARIE HARPOLD

A philosopher, ready to see the bright side of everything.

Commercial Club, '22; Girls' Glee Club, '22.

HELEN ADELE HARRIS

The world is as you take it.

Arion, '21, '22; Aristos, '22, '23; Science Club, '22, '23; Girls' Glee Club, '21, '22, '23; Operetta "Feast of the Little Lantern".

FRANCIS HARROLD

His muse is a spangled dancing girl.

E. ELIZABETH HARTMANN

She is fond of a healthy life, she is natural, unconventional.

Arion, '20, '21; Agora, '22, '23; Ethical Club, '23; Observer Staff, '22, '23; Pres. Agora, '23.

ADRIAN HATHAWAY

I admire a prompt person.

Class Baseball, '20, '21.

LAURA LOUISA HAUPT

Fancy doing all this by yourself! and without giving us notice!

MARTHA ANN HAWKINS

Women weaker than men? The idea!

Jr. Art League, '22, '23; Social Science Club, '22, '23.

HELEN M. HAYS

I want excitement—like the French Revolution.

Agora, '22, '23; Athletic Brd. of Control, '23; Class Basketball, '22, '23; Class Baseball, '22, '23; Hockey, '20, '22, '23; G. A. A., '20, '21, '22, '23; Tri-Y, '23; Hike Club, '22; Decanois Staff, '23.

JACK HENDERSON

Young men of spirit turn into solid men.

Mask & Wig, '22, '23; Rotaro, '20, '21, '22, '23; Hi-Y, '22, '23; "The Man Who Married a Dumb Wife"; "Such a Little Queen".

JEAN F. HENDERSON

God made women small in order to do a more perfect bit of workmanship.

G. A. A., '20.

EARL HETTINGER

I have that R. V. Winkle feeling.

LOUIS F. HIGGINS

He takes the world like daily bread, to be eaten, not talked about.

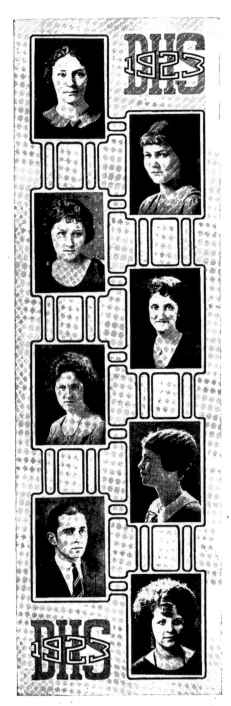

DOROTHY HILL

I know who you are. Perhaps you would like to know who I am?

MILDRED D. HILL

My brain is a perfect mill for projects.
Girls' Glee Club, '20, '21, '22, '23; Library Club, '20, '21, '22; Class Basketball, '19: G. A. A., '19.

NANCY HILL

She is cheerful and interesting.
Aristos, '22, '23; Class Basketball, '20, '21; G. A. A., '20, '21, '22, '23; Girls' Glee Club, '22, '23; Tri-Y, '23·

FERN HILL

Easy manners, unpretentious, natural behavior.

ANNA HINES

A harmonious character.
Aristos, '21, '22, '23; Commercial Club, '22, '23; Oikos, '21, '22·

IRENE HOFER

A lip as bright and rubious as Juno's own.

WILLIAM WALLACE HOGLE

He has a quick eye for a pretty ankle.
Jr. Art League, '23; Poster Club, '23; "Such a Little Queen"; Class Basketball, '20, '21, '22, '23; Class Baseball, '21·

VIRGINIA HOLMES

She has gentle blood in her veins.
Decanois Staff, '23·

BETTIE HOLT

She would admit none of the notorious errors of the world; its back biting, selfishness, intrusiveness.

Arion, '19; Decanois Staff, '23; Junior Observer, '22; Review Story Contest, '22.

WILLIARD S. HORNBACK

Mathematics is my very hip-bone.

GOLDIE MAE JOLLEY

Her name is a talisman.

EVELYNNE JONES

Her laugh strikes minor chords upon the heart strings.

Mask & Wig, '21, '22, '23; Tri-Y, '22, '23; Library Club, '20, '21; Class Basketball, '22; G. A. A., '21, '22, '23; "Spreading the News"; "The Play Goers".

MARGARET E. HUMPHREY

So completely is she mistress of herself.

Arion, '20, '21; Aristos, '22, '23; Mask & Wig, '20, '21, '22, '23; Pub. Spkg. Brd. of Control, '23; "The Tailor Made Man"; "The Man Who Married a Dumb Wife"; "Such a Little Queen"; Tri-Y, '23; Pres. of Mask & Wig, '23; Pres. of Aristos, '23.

ROY KASHNER

Genius is willing to lay the foundations of her structure unobserved.

Band, '19, '20, '22, '23; Forum, '23; Orchestra, '20, '23.

DORIS KELLEY

Life without freedom is not worth living.

Arion, '21, '22; Agora, '22, '23; Oikos, '21, '22; Social Science Club, '23; Class Basketball, '23; Class Baseball, '21, '22, '23; Hockey, '21, '22, '23; G. A. A., '21, '22, '23.

HOWARD KILE

He proved the best man on the field.

Athletic Brd. of Control, '22; Football, '21, '22, '23; "Such a Little Queen".

JESSIE KING

In great emergencies she can be sublime.

Aristos, '22, '23.

DAYLE V. KRETZINGER

He learns as if by intuition.

HELEN LOUISE KRUMSIEK

She's a prophet of a good omen.

Arion, '20, '21; Aristos, '22, '23; Orpheus, '21; Mask & Wig, '21, '22, '23; Girls' Glee Club, '22, '23; G. A. A., '23; "The Tailor Made Man"; "No Smoking"; "Two Crooks and a Lady".

MARGARET LANCASTER

Lovable people are seldom, nay, never perfect.

Arion, '20, '21; Agora, '22, '23; Hockey, '21, '22; Class Basketball, '22, '23; G. A. A., '20, '21, '22, '23; Girls' Glee Club, '22, '23; Tri-Y, '22, '23; Pres. of Girls' Athletic Association, '23; Music Memory Contest, '21.

RENA B. LANDERS

Tears are shed for other things than the gift of gold.

Girls' Glee Club, '23.

PAUL WALLACE LEWIS

I have learned that men and women are like plants; to be useful they must be rooted firmly in their own soil.

Athletic Brd. of Control, '22, '23; Football, '21, '22.

GUY WESLEY LITTERST

His eyes look right through a man's skull, no matter how thick it is.

Boys' Glee Club, '22, '23; Poster Club, '20, '21; Social Science Club, '22.

SELMA LUCILLE LIVELY

I can do more by myself.

Jr. Art League, '21; Poster Club, '22; Social Science Club, '22, '23.

MINNIE L. LUNSFORD

My domain is out in the open, with the sun.

Commercial Club, '22, '23; Class Basketball, '21, '22; G. A. A., '21, '22, '23; Tri-Y, '22, '23.

PERLEY LUPTON

The debate is the very breath of my nostrils.

Forum, Pres. '23; Science Club, '22, (pres.) '23; Observer Staff; Debate, '23; "Such a Little Queen".

LOUISE LYONS

The hue of truth is in her character.

GLADYS MACDONALD

She would never cry for the moon.

Jr. Art League, '22; Poster Club, '22; Hockey, '20; G. A. A., '19, '20, '21; Girls' Glee Club, '22.

NETA FLORA MAFFIT

She loves the delicate slopes of a hillside.

EDNA MARTIN

A vivid person.

M. FERNE MARTIN

I am steering my little craft.

Orchestra, '19, '20, '21.

NELIUS B. MARTIN

Viewed impersonally the world is a rattling good show.

Arion, '19; Agora, '21, '22, '23; Science Club, '22, '23; Girls' Glee Club, '22, '23; Hockey, '21, '22; G. A. A., '20, '21, '22, '23; Tri-Y, '22, '23.

LOUISE MASON

*Will you know the fatal magnetism I exert
over fossils.*

Agora, '22, '23; G. A. A., '23.

V. FERN McCOLLUM

*Most of her actions are committed under
the dictation of her heart, not her head.*

ARTHUR McCRAY

Humor has the greatest power for good.

JOHN W. McDONALD

Gay men find the smiling climate.

Class Baseball, '21.

GENEVA McRILL

*She has a wish to go to South America
and see the Amazon.*

JOHN W. MEARA

I may be dashed to smithereens.

VIOLA MELTON

A modern Priscilla.

Arion, '20, '21; Aristos, '21, '22, '23; Ethical
Club, '22, '23; Mask & Wig, '21, '22, '23;
"'Op O' My Thumb"; "The Turtle Dove".

CORA MICHENER

You'd rhapsodize with her.

Arion, '20; Agora, '21, '22; Commercial
Club, '22, '23; Oikos, '21; Class Basketball,
'21, '22; Class Baseball, '21, '22, '23; Track
'20; Hockey '20, '21, '22; G. A. A., '20, '21,
'22, '23; Hike Club, '20, '21, '22, '23; Tri-Y,
'22, '23; Girls' Glee Club, '21, '22.

MYRNA OLIVE MILLER

It is delightful to see anything done well.
Oikos, '20·

CHESTER MILLIGAN

Nobody knows it but you, me and the Bamboo tree.

LOUISE E. MILNES

I· have the satisfaction of knowing that I have stuck to my post.
Aristos, '22, '23; Ethical Club, '22, '23; Social Science Club, '22, '23·

J. HAROLD MINTUN

He could tell you many interesting things.

RUTH DOROTHY MOESSNER

I'm doing my best to keep things bright within.
Class Basketball, '19; Class Baseball, '19; Hockey, '19; G. A. A., '20·

MARGARET MOONEY

From this day I'm going to give full rein to my fancy.

SARA FRANCES MOORE

I will kick a few kicks before I disappear.
Commercial Club, '23.

FLORENCE MOOTHART

I'm not made of stuff that runs.

GLENN MULLIKIN

Out of the harness again, and glad of it.

MAURICE N. MUNCH

His eyes constantly scour the horizon.

Boys' Glee Club, '22, '23.

ARTHUR MURPHY

Ibsen said, "This is a man's world!"

"Ag." Club, '20, '21; Class Basketball, '23; Football, '20; Varsity, '21.

EARL F. MYERS

I'm planning a wild career of self-indulgence.

Band, '22, '23; Class Basketball, '20, '21, '22, '23; Class Baseball, '19, '20; Track, '21.

RUTH VIOLA MYERS

You think I'm pulling for shore, but I'm not.

Girls' Glee Club, '22, '23.

RAY NEWLIN

Perhaps you would have different impressions of things if you saw them through my spectacles.

Band, '22, '23; Boys' Glee Club, '20, '21, '22, '23; Orchestra, '23; "The Trial by Jury".

WILLIAM NICHOLSON

I've known plenty of magic eyes.

Boys' Glee Club, '22, '23; Observer Staff; Football, '22.

FREEDA OLIVE

The best and most important thing in the world is folks.

Commercial Club, '23.

CLARENCE PATTENGALE

I'm everlastingly through with love and sentiment.

RUTH IRENE PATTERSON

It's an old fable that love is blind.

ROLLIN PEASE

My energy is spasmodic.

Band, '21, '22, '23; Forum, '21, '22, '23; Orchestra, '19, '20, '21, '22, '23; Orpheus, '21, '22; Science Club, '21, '22; Commencement Program.

L. ELWOOD PENSINGER

I'm not seasick, just popular.

Class Basketball, '19, '20; Varsity Baseball, '21; Class Baseball, '20, '21; Track, '21.

WILLIAM PITNER

He has a poise that men envy.

Mask & Wig, '21, '22, '23; Rotaro, '23; Decanois Staff; "The Tailor Made Man"; "Two Crooks and a Lady"; "The Man Who Married a Dumb Wife"; "Such a Little Queen".

VIVIAN CAROLYN POLLOCK

Things must be done on the stroke of the clock.

Arion, '20, '21; Mask & Wig, '21, '22, '23; Library Club, '20; Observer Staff; "No Smoking".

FANNY POWERS

Clever in many ways, and good to look at.

Arion, '21; Aristos, '22, '23; Decanois Staff.

HERMAN PRITCHETT

His head is simply spinning with plans.

Mask & Wig, '21, '22, '23; Rotaro, '20, '21, '22, '23; Science Club, '22, '23; Decanois Staff, '23; "The Man Who Married a Dumb Wife"; "Such a Little Queen"; "Spreading the News"; "Debate, '22, '23; Silver Delta, '21.

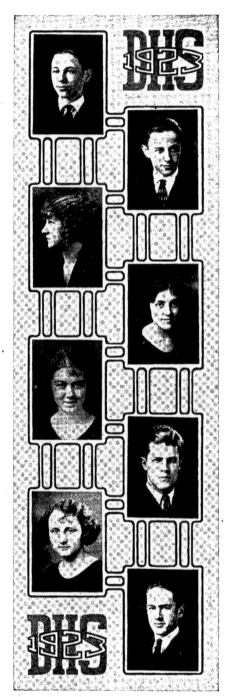

DONALD O. PYGMAN

Do you wonder that he almost danced a hole in the parlor rug,

Band, '22, '23; Orchestra, '21, '23.

DURWARD B. PYGMAN

Think what I might have done!

Band, '22; Rotaro, '21, '22.

LUCILLE QUICKEL

Manners and courtesy come natural to her.

Athletic Brd. of Control, '22, '23; Class Basketball, '23; Hockey, '20, '23; G. A. A., '20, '23.

GRACE OTHEL RAFFE

For a steady diet I can stand the saints much better than the sinners.

Girls' Glee Club, '22, '23.

ENID RAGAN

Of course we all know that she is the salt of the earth.

Arion, '20, '21; Aristos, '21, '22; Oikos, '20; Orpheus, '20, '21, '22; Girls' Glee Club, '21, '22.

JAMES RATTAN

He has the finest natural gifts I ever saw.

Rotaro, '21; Observer Staff, '22 Decanois Staff, '23; Varsity Basketball, 24; Class Basketball, '19, '21; Football, '21; "Such a Little Queen"; Junior Class President; Student Council, '22, '23; (pres. '22, '23); Salutatorian.

ARA RAWLINGS

I'm absolutely walking on air today.

Commercial Club, '23; G. A. A., '23.

EARL RAY

But to think of all my ambitions and aspirations!

Forum, '22; Science, '22, '23.

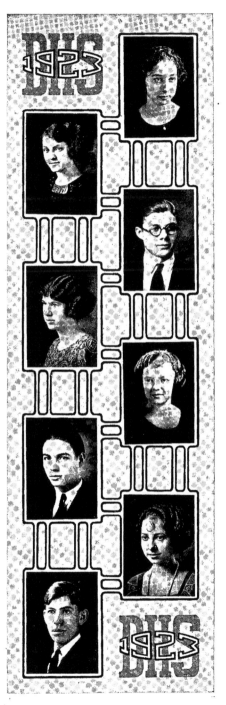

ANNA MAY RHODERICK
What strange things human beings are!

LORINE RHODES
She can do many things well and likes them all.
Agora, '22, '23; Orchestra, '22, '23.

EARL . RICHARDSON
Hale and hearty.
Varsity Basketball, '22, '23; Football, '22.

MILDRED JUNE RICKETTS
What a wonderful day!
Girls' Glee Club, '21, '22, '23; Jr. Art League, '22; Poster Club, '22; Class Basketball, '21; Hockey, '21, '22; G. A. A. '21, '22; President of Girls' Glee Club, '23.

MARGARET ALICE RIVES
I haven't time to be lonely.
Arion, '20, '21; Aristos, '21, '22, '23; Oikos, '20; Mask & Wig, '21.

WILLIAM ROBINSON, JR.
He's so strange and picturesque.

MARGARET L. ROMANUS
Before everything else she is an optimist.
Observer Staff, '22, '23; Arion, '20, '21; Hockey, '20, '21; G. A. A., '20, '21.

JOSEPH ROSENBERG
He is strong in aggression, strong in defense.
Rotaro, '22, '23; Class Basketball, '20; "Such a Little Queen"; Decanois Staff, '23.

LUCILLE RYMAN

Life interests me for its ease, its charm, its humor and its loveliness.

ANGELINE PRISCILLA SALING

Now let's be sociable.

Agora, '22' '23; Girls' Glee Club, '22' '23; Ethical Club, '22' '23; Science Club, '22; Social Science Club, '22' '23; Hockey, '22.

FREDA MARIE SANDERS

A great deal of preliminary intelligence.

Arion, '21' '22; Commercial Club, '22' '23; Girls' Glee Club, '21' '22; Library Club, '21; Pres. Arion, '21; Tri-Y, '22' '23.

ANDREW SANTANEN

His outlook is essentially sane, essentially normal.

Forum, '22; Science Club, '22; Class Baseball, '19.

KATHERINE SCHNEIDERS

The sun that melts my heart will have to rise in the west.

Class Baseball, '21.

HARRY SCHROEDER

I don't want to discomboberete anyone.

RAYMOND W. SCHULZ

Born into a world of many unsettled problems.

Orchestra, '20' '22.

ESTHER SCRANTON

She put on her robes of philosophy to cloak discouragement.

Arion, '19; Jr. Art League, '22' '23; Poster Club, '22' '23; Observer Staff; Decanois Staff; Pres. of Poster Club, '23.

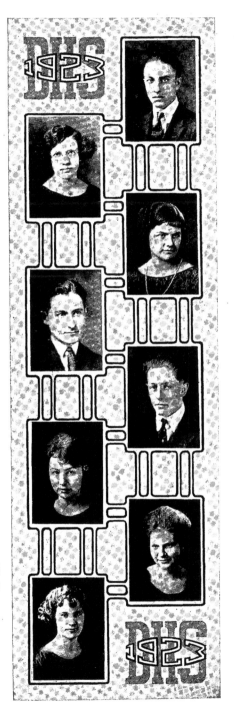

NORMAN A. SCRANTON

He never acknowledged a trouble; he dispersed it.

"Ag" Club, '22.

HELEN L. SCURLOCK

She's not the kind you can ask personal questions of.

Orchestra, '20, '21, '22, '23.

FRANCES C. SELLARS

She had a nature as sparkling as sea foam.

Aristos, '21, '22; Jr. Art League, '22, '23; Oikos, '20, '21; Poster Club, '22, '23.

LORENZO C. SHAFFER

A ship with a wide channel ahead.

Band, '17, '18, '22, '23; Orchestra, '17, '18, '22, '23; Orpheus, '22.

RICHARD SHIRK

I hate poetry.

Band, '19, '21, '22, '23.

DOROTHY SHAW

She had an idea, she had captured Fortune.

Arion, '20, '21; Aristos, '21, '22, '23; Girls' Glee Club, '21, '22, '23; Oikos, '21, '22; Hockey, '21, '22; G. A. A., '21, '22, '23; Tri-Y, '22, '23; Library Club, '20, (pres.) '21; Orpheus, '20, '21, '22.

ELEANOR SHAW

She is composed.

Arion, '20, '21; Aristos, '22, '23; Jr. Art League, '23; Orpheus, '20, '21, '22; Girls' Glee Club, '23; Tri-Y, '22, '23; Hockey, '23; G. A. A., '22, '23.

RUTH SHELTON

Her smile was quite unclouded.

Girls' Glee Club, '22, '23.

GRACE SHIELDS

Perhaps when I am old and wrinkled I'll be at peace.

Girls' Glee Club, '23·

ROBERTA SHIELDS

She has a first-hand acquaintance with the compact.

Aristos, '22· '23; Class Basketball, '20· '21· '22· '23; Class Baseball, '20· '21· '22; Track, '20; Hockey, '20· '21· '22· '23; G. A. A., '20· '21· '22· '23; Social Science Club, '22· '23; Observer Staff, '23; Girls' Glee Club, '22· '23; Tri-Y, '22· '23; Pres. of Girls' Glee Club, '22; President of Tri-Y, '23·

MILDRED EUGENIA SIMONDS

I'm a new person in a new world.

Girls' Glee Club, '22· '23; Class Baseball, '18· '19; Hockey, '18· '19; G. A. A., '19· '20· '21·

MARGARET MAE SIMONS

A worker, always doing her level best.

Aristos, '23; Ethical Club, '23; Social Science Club, '23; "Such a Little Queen".

RUSSELL SIX

He treats old and young with a sure touch and in the kindest manner.

Forum, '22; Junior Class Officer.

HELEN M. SKINNER

I have mingled with men and with little pleasure.

Aristos, '22· '23; Ethical Club, '22·

DOROTHY M. SLEETER

To think of being reduced to a curly head and a pair of wings!

Girls' Glee Club, '22· '23.

ZOLA ELIZABETH SLOAN

She knows the sweet weariness that comes after work.

Aristos, '21· '22· '23; Ethical Club, '22· '23; Social Science Club, '22· '23; Debate, '22; Observer, '22· '23; Pres. of Aristos, '22; Review Story Contest, '21; Silver Delta '21; Health Contest, '21; Girls' Glee Club, '21· '22·

FLORENCE SPOONER

She has a masculine respect for her word.

BERNARD STODDART

I like to act bored.

JOHN STOUGH, JR.

Oh! the softening effects of love!

Boys' Glee Club, '22, '23.

GENEVIEVE WELLS STOUT

Her name is always on the honor roll.

MILDRED STOUTENBOROUGH

She's as dainty as Ophelia.

Science Club, '22, '23; G. A. A., '21, '22, '23; "The Turtle Dove".

CLARA SULLIVAN

It is the third dimention that gives illusion-ment to life.

Oikos, '21.

VERNA MAUDE SUTTON

If overcoming difficulties makes character, then I will have as many characters as the Chinese alphabet.

Ethical Club; '22, '23; Social Science Club, '22, '23; Pres. of Ethical Club, '22.

RASSELE SWARTHOUT

He has the grand gesture.

Forum, '21, '22, '23; Mask & Wig, '21, '22, '23; Debate, '22; Athletic Association, '22; "Trial by Jury"; "Tailor Made Man"; 'Such a Little Queen".

RUTH C. SWARTHOUT

She looks sideways; of course, you might speak to her.

MARTHA TROUTMAN

How magnanimous she is!

CECILIA F. UHL

Benignly disposed towards all creation.

MILDRED VERNER

Her smile is better than her frown.
Hockey, '20; G. A. A., '20·

BEATRICE E. VICK

A quiet stream runs deepest.
Commercial Club, '23; Ethical Club, '23·

HAZEL R. VIRDEN

I have learned life's deepest lesson here.
Ethical Club, '22· '23·

MARSHALL WAGGONER

That's an idea I can't cuddle up to.

RUTH WALDEN

There's surely Saxon in her blood.
Arion, '21; Aristos, '22· '23; Mask & Wig, '23; Social Science Club, '22; Observer Staff, '23; "Turtle Dove"; "The Feast of the Little Lanterns".

ANNA E. WALKER

She is adept with a paint brush.

Jr. Art League, '22, '23; Poster Club, '22, '23; Tri-Y, '23.

CHESTER WALKER

He radiates good cheer wherever he goes.

Rotaro, '21, '22, '23; Band, '21, '22, '23; (Pres. '22, '23); Boys' Glee Club, '20, '21, '22, '23; (Pres. '22, '23).

THOMAS WALSH

Words seem such inadequate things.

Forum, '23.

CONSTANCE WALTZ

Vision and ardor constitute her merit.

Arion, '19, '20, '21; Aristos, '21, '22, '23; Orpheus, '22; Observer Staff, '21; Silver Delta, '21; Pres of Arion, '21.

CLARA ELIZABETH WARNES

She says little, but leaves one wondering; therefore she is charming.

ELIZABETH WARREN

She has repose and good will.

Girls' Glee Club, '21.

RUBY A. WASSON

Her passions were absolutely in harmony with her intelligence.

Jr. Art League, '22, '23; Poster Club, '22, '23; Girls' Glee Club, '22, '23; Class Basketball, '20, '21.

NELLIE B. WEBER

We like your disposition, your friendship, n' everything.

Orpheus, '21, '22; Science Club, '22, '23; G. A. A., '21, '22, '23; Decanois Staff, '23; Tri-Y, '23.

ERMA WHITSETT

Ladies never attempt to be perfect.

Arion, '21·

JANICE IRENE WIDICK

As hard to please as Cleopatra at sixteen.

Arion, '20· '21'; Aristos, '21· '22· '23; Poster Club, '20· '21· '22· '23; Decanois Staff, '23.

ANNA WILLIAMS

She is obliging and amiable.

WILLARD E. WILLIAMS

He has brains, not ledger-keeping, duck-hunting brains, but imagination.

Rotaro, '23; Class Basketball, '21·

LAWRENCE H. WITT

I get the worth of my money.

Band, '23; Orchestra, '23; Rotaro, '22· '23·

EVERETT B. WITZEMAN

With her at his side, nothing is impossible to him.

Band, '22· '23; Boys' Glee Club, '22· '23; Rotaro, '22· '23; Hi-Y, '20· '21· '22· '23; Decanois Staff, '23; Pres. of Rotaro, '23·

ELEANOR LOUISE WOOD

Her pure and eloquent blood spoke in her cheeks.

Arion, '20; Aristos, '21· '22·

FLOYD C. WYKOFF

Success, is to leave nothing to chance.

Band, '21; '22; '23; Mask & Wig, '21; Observer, '22; Varsity Basketball, '21; Class Baseball, '21· '22·

SIDNEY ROSENTHAL

Even tho' vanquished, he could argue still.

Debate, '23; Forum, '23·

ALBERTA ZEFF

Petite et pleine de vie.

Commercial Club, '22, '23; Jr. Art League, '22; Social Science Club, '23·

.RAE SAYRE

The world is as you take it.

Boys' Glee Club, '21, '23; Football, '20, '21; Class aseball, '19, '20, '21; Class Basketball, '18.

ERICK WINTER

I wonder if he thinks as much. as he talks.

Rotaro, '22, '23·; Debate, '22, '23·

Commencement Program

Invocation· ....

Salutatory ....James Rattan

Piano Solo ....Henrietta Clark

Reading ....Margaret Humphrey

Learned Oration ....Merrill De Baum

Cornet Solo ....Rollin Pease

Valedictory ....Glenn McClelland

AWARDS

Certificates

Diplomas

Scholarship

Mary W. French

Deltas

Ida K. Martin

Benediction ....

Salutatorian and Valedictorian

The salutatorian, James Rattan, has been especially active in class affairs for the last two years. In his junior year he was chosen class president and under his leadership and aggressiveness much was accomplished. He worked hard and spent much time in preparing and finishing work, which never failed. His senior year has far surpassed his junior year. Last spring the faculty chose him as business manager for the 1923 Decanois. He has been a capable and reliable manager and has originated many new ideas and carried them out successfully. He has served on several committees of the Senior Class, the most important being the Ring and Pin Committee. James was active in football and basketball and has been an all-around student.

The faculty conferred the honor of Valedictorian upon Glenn McClelland, president of the Senior Class, and they made no mistake in this action. Glenn was formerly a member of Rotaro, the leading boy's literary society of the school, and when he served as vice-president, it was felt that he was one of the best vice-presidents the society ever has had. In 1922 he represented D. H. S. in the Charleston Oratorical Contest. He held down an end position of the football team last fall and was one of the high point men in the interclass track meet this spring. He is an all A student and as president of the Senior Class has showed his ability and willingness to work in all undertakings.

The Class of 1923 should be proud to have two of the best and most prominent members of the class as Salutatorian and Valedictorian.

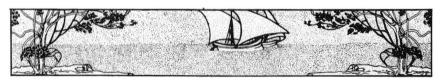

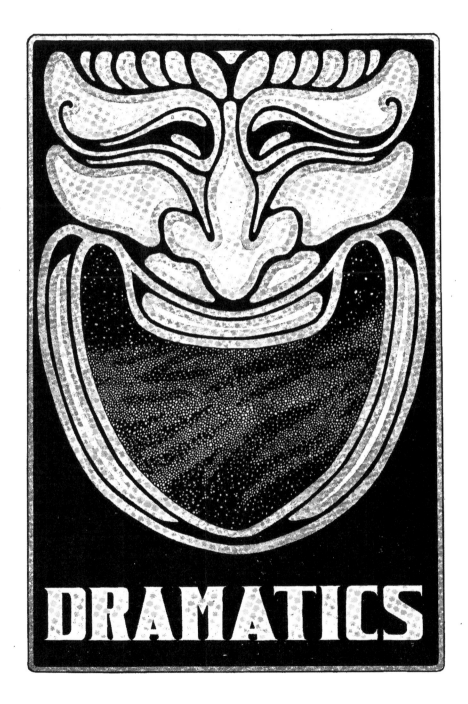

Top Row—Fessler, Wicklein, Lutz, Hill, Wait, Pritchett, Henderson.
Second Row—Regan, Abell, Evans, Chaille, Pollock.
Third Row—Heil, Barnett, Adams, Pitner, Rhodes, Walden.
Bottom Row—Busch, Beckold, Danzeisen (Pres.), Swarthout, Humphrey, Krumsiek.

Mask and Wig Dramatic Club

Officers

	First Semester	Second Semester
President	MARGARET HUMPHREY	EUGENE DANZEISEN
Vice-President	ERMINA BUSCH	VIVIAN POLLOCK
Secretary	BONNIE REGAN	HERMAN PRITCHETT
Treasurer	WILLIAM PITNER	WILLIAM PITNER
Sergeant-at-Arms	{ EUGENE DANZEISEN / VIOLA MELTON	JACK HENDERSON / RASSELE SWARTHOUT
Press Reporter	MAURINE EVANS	BERNICE BECKOLD

Members 1922-1923

Annie Adams
Ruth Ackerman
Charles Barnard
Esther Barnett
Bernice Beckold
Tom Bohon
Ermina Busch
Lucille Chaille
Florence Coles
Eugene Danzeisen
Carolyn Drennan
Margaret Duggan

Ernest Earle
Edna Espy
Maurine Evans
Goldie Fessler
Frank Gollings
Francis Harrold
John Heil
Jack Henderson
Princess Hill
Margaret Humphrey
Evelynne Jones
Helen Krumsiek

Daniel Lutz
Viola Melton
William Pitner
Vivian Pollock
Herman Pritchett
Bonnie Regan
Olive Rhodes
Rassele Swarthout
Franklin Wait
Ruth Walden
Ruth Wicklein

The Man Who Married a Dumb Wife

On the night of January 5, 1923 Mask and Wig presented its master production "The Man Who Married a Dumb Wife" by Anatole France. Under the able direction of Miss Eliza Thomas, this play which is shunned by most directors of amateur productions because of its severe demands upon the actors, was a brilliant success. The parts were all exceptionally well taken. The cast was as follows:

Giles Boiscourtier ....Herman Pritchett
The Chickweed Man ....Frank Gollings
Alison, Botal's Servant ....Ermina Busch
Master Adam Fumee, Lawyer ....Franklin Wait
Master Leonard Botal, Judge ....William Pitner
The Water Cress Man ....Vernard Poland
The Candle Man ....Daniel Lutz
Catherine, Botal's Wife ....Bernice Beckold
A Blind Fiddler ....Ruth Wicklein
Chimney Sweep ....John Heil
Master Simon Colline ....Eugene Danzeisen
Master Jean Maugier ....Charles Barnard
Surgeon's Attendants ....Charles Schaub, Ernest Earle
Master Serafin Dulaurier, Apothecary ....Rassele Swarthout
Page to Madame de la Bruine..............Jack Henderson
Madame de la Bruine ....Edna Espy
Mademoiselle de la Garandier ....Margaret Humphrey

Such a Little Queen

"Such a Little Queen" by Channing Pollock was presented by the senior class with great success. Bonnie Regan, the sweet and true little exiled queen, did a splendid piece of work and the audience all agreed with the king when he called her "such a little queen". A young and carefree king who developed into a serious minded and true king was admirably shown by Glenn McClelland.

Baron Cosaca, a dignified royalist and diplomat, forced to manual labor by loyalty to his queen was portrayed well by Eugene Danzeisen. The difficult part of A. D. Lauman, the stern and self-made business man was well taken by William Pitner. "Lissie" Lauman otherwise Margaret Humphrey played well a gracious and lovely American girl. Roy Brady was good as a rising American youth.

Mary, the Irish maid, played by Mae Simons and Nathaniel Quigg, the hard-hearted landlord, played by James Rattan, furnished the audience with true humor.

General Myrza, powerful and conceited, was well taken by Rassele Swarthout. Other members of the royal embassy were well done by Carl Goodwin, Perley Lupton, Wallace Hogle and Charles Barnard. Montford Collins acted the part of the villian very well and Jack Henderson brought a laugh with his "bit".

The wonderful work is greatly appreciated of "the lady behind the scenes", Miss Thomas who "makes this play possible". The orchestra furnished enjoyable music between acts and thanks is due them. All these cooperated to make "Such a Little Queen" the "best ever" class play.

Mary . . . . Mae Simons
Ice Man . . . . Lester Foltz
Baron Cosaca, Prime Minister of Herzogovina. . Eugene Danzeisen

Anna, Queen of Herzogovina .... Bonnie Regan
Butcher's Boy .... Herman Pritchett
Nathaniel Quigg .... James Rattan
Robert Trainor .... Roy Brady
A. D. Lauman .... William Pitner
Elizabeth Lauman .... Margaret Humphrey
Stephen IV, King of Bosnia .... Glenn McClelland
Cora Fitzgerald .... Dorothy Wilson
Margaret Donnelly .... Ermina Busch
Harry Sherman .... Montford Collins
Porter .... Howard Kile
A Messenger .... Jack Henderson
Count Mavichic .... Charles Barnard
General Myrza .... Rassele Swarthout
Hale .... Carl Goodwin
Colonel Haupt .... Perley Lupton
Prince Niklas .... Wallace Hogle

Two Crooks and a Lady

"Two Crooks and a Lady", a short one-act play by Eugene Pillot was
presented under the direction of Miss Thomas on Thursday evening, September 28, 1922 before the Parent-Teachers Association of the High School.
Excellent work, characteristic of all the Mask and Wig productions, was
manifest throughout the play. The cast was as follows:

Miller, the Hawk ....Charles Barnard
Lucille ....Ermina Busch
Miss Jones ....Maurine Evans
Police Inspector ....Rassele Swarthout
Garrity, a policeman ....William Pitner
Mrs. Summens-Vance ....Helen Krumsiek

No Smoking

As a curtain-raiser for "The Man Who Married a Dumb Wife", Mask
and Wig presented "No Smoking", a one-act comedy by Jacinto Benvente.
The actors took their parts in a way that delighted the large and appreciative
audience. Miss Helen Krumsiek especially distinguished herself by her portrayal of feminine talkativeness. The cast was as follows:

A Lady ....Helen Krumsiek
A Young Lady ....Vivian Pollock
A Gentleman ....Tom Bohon
A Conductor ....Frank Rowdybusch

Spreading the News

An Irish comedy, "Spreading the News", written by Lady Gregory was presented in the auditorium on Friday, October 20, 1922. The play dealt with the spreading of gossip by an old, deaf, apple-woman. This delightful one-act play was much enjoyed by the High School students. Each member of the cast took his part well. The cast is as follows:

Bartley Fallon	William Pitner
Mrs. Fallon	Florence Coles
Mrs. Tully	Helen Clayton
Mrs. Tarpey	Evelyn Jones
Jack Smith	Tom Bohon
James Ryan	Franklin Wait
Shaun Early	Ernest Earle
Tim Casey	Eugene Danzeisen
A Policeman, Joe Muldoon	Frank Rowdybusch
A Removable Magistrate	Frank Gollings

Turtle Dove

"Turtle Dove", a clever two-act Chinese play was presented in the auditorium Monday, November 27, 1922 by Mask and Wig. The play was enacted in the Chinese manner without stage effects and with a chorus to announce the story. The costumes were attractive, and the acting was characteristic of excellent work done by the dramatic club under the supervision of the advisor, Miss Eliza Thomas. The cast was as follows.

Chorus	Ruth Ackerman
Chong-Tut-Yen, son of Chong	Edna Espy
Won-Yiu	Ruler of Canton
Mandarin	Ruth Walden
Kiven Tiu, his daughter	Viola Melton
God of Fate	Mildred Stoutenborough
Property Man	Ruth Wicklien
Song Bearer	Florence Coles

Irish Stew

The wheels of the heavily loaded box car grated and squeaked as they click-clacked over the steel rails. It was one o'clock in the afternoon. We— Stupe and I, looked far off at the horizon where the great Black Hawk mountains loomed up against the clear sky. The mountains were black and purple and a mist hung over them, giving them a cool, moist look. But even as we gazed and marvelled at their grandeur we noticed the strange, dusty taste in our already parched mouths and throats. It was from the great alkali plain that stretched between us and the mountains, some thirty or thirty-five miles. It was a new sight to us. Nothing but sand—sand with its cacti— with its scrubbing sage brush. The view itself was enough to make a person uncomfortably warm—but—there was a breeze blowing; not the kind of breeze that one usually calls to mind, no indeed. It was like that from an oven; it was as if a great fan had been placed in a furnace and we were sitting stupidly in front of the open door. It was warm, yes very warm; in fact it was hot. Stupe looked at me and bestowed on me a smile that said, "Its mighty hot, but we don't mind; do we, kid?" I smiled back my answer of, "No, we kind of enjoy it some way or other. We don't want everything to be just right."

Neither had spoken a word, yet we both understood, and consequently both sat there content at slowly being burned to a crisp.

But this could not go on forever. The old sid-wheeled "Q" engine gave three shrieks such as a great monster might have produced at seeing water after such a pull through that blazing plain. At sound of the whistle we both leaped to our feet—our eyes glowing with joy; we had forgotten the heat and the scenery. We knew what it meant—it meant an oasis. We scrambled down from the observation platform of our side-door pullman. We could smell the steel-brake shoes burning as they made it their business to stop the on coming procession of freight.

Here was water—we could have all we wished—yet we stood there grinning at one another as lunatics might have grinned at seeing a burning building. We were not exactly crazy however; we were only contemplating the joy and strength we would get from the drink. When finally we had washed the dust and torrid atmosphere from our mouths, we did not drink much, three or four swallows probably. Not that that was all we wanted—no—I could have gulped down a quart of the refreshing stuff without taking a breath; but that would never do, for we had two more hours of heat before the sun would get low and the cool breezes from the mountains and the desert would be upon us.

The rest of the afternoon passed quietly. Now and then a monstrous jack-rabbit would jump up and race the train for a hundred yards, or a snake would crawl lazily from under a cactus only to crawl back again in disgust at the sun; or in a stagnant pool a turtle would be sleeping on a stone or a log.

We were not bothered any more from lack of water. We only looked at the scenery as the low freight swung along the curving track. We were coming into the foothills now. On the east rose high cliffs, and on some were vivid red spots which we soon discovered were shale. It was unusually red, blood red—and reminded one of an enormous open wound on the side of a giant.

We looked back down the tracks; there it lay—a great swerving, graceful path that lay between great hills of rock and sand. We could see and trace its course for miles.

We were becoming tired. Hunger had begun to tell us the time of day. We had been riding all day and it was now nearly six o'clock. The jolt and twist of the car seemed to get more and more tiresome; it seemed to shake us up as if we were on the ocean. We were empty. I felt like a boiler with some nice sharp stones being shaken inside. I dreamed of great tender steaks, good crisp potatoes and even of a great traditional Thanksgiving turkey with all its trimmings and sauces. But to my dismay these thoughts seemed only to make my condition worse. I looked at Stupe—my pal—he was going off into the distant fleecy clouds that crowned the sky line. His face had changed; he too was hungry. But as he turned toward me he smiled. He always smiled—and I smiled too. We always smiled. We were happy—we didn't mind being hungry for a time. It would only make our next meal more enjoyable.

The train was gaining speed rapidly. We were going down a grade. The engine whistled four times. The brakes began to take hold with a grinding, screeching noise. We were assured we were coming to a town. Yes, it was the division of the railroad. It was Gillette, Wyoming.

We hopped off at a grade crossing that looked as if it might lead to town. We walked hurriedly. Our sides ached with hunger; they felt as if they were on the verge of caving it. Suddenly Stupe gave a gleeful little chuckle and verred off to the left, grabbing me and dragging me in his wake as he did so. It was a little lunch car that had caught his eye. It was barely high enough for a man to stand up in and there were only about five seats along an old rough counter.

We flopped down on two of the seats with such a thud that it seemed we would never again get up. We rasped our dirty hands together and prepared for the deluge. The proprietor was already ladling something into some bowls and as he swung them up on the counter, he called in a loud warning, "Irish Stew!"

It was Irish Stew all right, but not exactly the kind we had ever seen before. In the middle of the bowl was a great portion of "bully" beef. It was swimming in a liquid that resembled to a very great degree—rich dish water. But the meat was not alone for as I inhaled that heavenly stuff, I encountered—potatoes, corn, celery leaves, carrotts, cabbage, beans and anything else that any one might wish to add. But it was delicious, or at least it seemed such to me at that time, and I did not stop with one—but it took two of those enormous receptacles full of the steaming stuff to appease my hunger.

I have thought back many times and have seen that same piece of meat and those vegetables of every variety floating around in that gray-green liquid—and thought how much, many people have missed by never being really hungry.

LESTER FOLTZ.

A Maid and a Mirror

Breathes there a girl with soul so dead, who never to herself hath said, "If my nose were only——"? The maid with a short, saucy nose sighs for one of dignified proportions, and vice versa. Were it not for that combined friend and enemy of feminity, the mirror, the multitudes of women struggling for beauty would be blissfully ignorant of their various facial imperfections.

Perhaps some day a poet will put into verse the great Quest of the Ages, namely, the search for Beauty. Women have sighed for, cried for, and even died for that quality possessed by so few and desired by so many. Indeed, we may liken these ladies unto Launfals in search of the Golden Grail of Pulchritude. With the advent of mirrors, peace departed from the soul of woman, and the struggle was on.

Imagine the state of mind of the first woman who saw her reflection in a bit of silvered glass, especially if she had been wrongly led to believe she possessed a perfect profile. My heart goes out to her departed spirit if she discovered, as I did, that her nose was inclined to point skyward. If she were a sensible creature, she refused to surrender to a cruel fate, and set about to remedy the defect. No doubt her grandchildren are now engaged in similar occupations by maintaining Marinello shops, if we believe what scientists tell us about heredity.

In this modern age, woman is constantly surrounded by references to her beauty, or to her lack of it. People who profess to be humane, write lengthy instructions on the achievements of beauty, which generally begin; "Take your mirror in hand and study your face carefully, especially the side views." I said "profess" because no true humanitarian would voluntarily cause so much misery as do the above instructions. There is little doubt that the old proverb, "Ignorance is bliss", must have been coined by some victim of similar advice. There is no other word which so aptly describes the poor creature heeding the words, "Take your mirror in hand", as victim. I know, for I write from experience.

.How well do I remember that day when I read those fatal, soul-destroying words! A great desire to be a famous beauty assailed me, and as there was no one near to warn me of the trials and heartaches ambushed along the road to Comliness, I set out on the journey. I confidently expected soon to join the ranks of Venus, Cleopatra, Helen of Troy, and Mary Pickford. Those of my readers who are more sophisticated will no doubt smile superciliously, but let them bear in mind that I was young and gullible. There were advertisements, articles, illustrations and talks to encourage me in my pursuit, and as I reasoned (while under the influence of a saying, "It is every girl's right to be beautiful") I might as well try it, anyhow.

I began with a wonderful preparation called Facial Clay, or something equally as bad. It was positively guaranteed to produce flawless beauty at the end of a forty-minute application. I tried it, but the results were not what they should have been. I consoled myself by suggesting that perhaps I had not discovered just which forty minutes the instructions called for. The next attempt was made a day later while the family was not at home. Don't think I am furtive or anything like that, but I deemed it wiser to keep my project secret, as I knew from past experience that the family was hopelessly uneducated along similar lines. To proceed, I assembled the accessories to the act, namely; a bowl of ice, a kettle of boiling water, numerous towels, and last but not least, *the* soap. Even now I can see that weird greenish color of that soap, and smell its peculiar odor of violets, gasoline and garlic. I followed directions, even until I came to the place where I was to, "massage the facial muscles with ice, then dash the boiling water on the skin". I may have had the directions misquoted or backwards, but the effects were just the same, and were all that the manufacturer had claimed they would be, especially the bright glowing color which would be restored. I had that part all right, for I glowed like a boiled lobster. All the effects were not beneficial, however. Father wanted to call the doctor for a severe case of hives, and Mother wept bitter tears over my "ruined countenance". I gradually recovered, both mentally and physically, though the mental cure was effected first. I firmly resolved, while gazing at my swollen, distorted face, that the end didn't justify the means.

DOROTHY WILSON.

Dogs

Dogs are dogs. There are big dogs, little dogs, fat dogs, lean dogs, long dogs, short dogs, wooly dogs, smooth dogs, long-eared dogs, short-tailed dogs, amiable dogs, surly dogs, pretty dogs, ugly dogs, barking dogs and biting dogs, yet they are all dogs—creatures entirely different from any other animal.

Was there ever a boy who did not like dogs? As we advance along the pathway of life, we may grow away from the early love of this cosmopolitan animal, but even then there are few of us who can resist the attraction of a rolly-polly puppy, playing with its brothers and sisters in the soap box which it knows as home, while near by its mother dozes watchfully. Never is domestic tranquillity more perfectly expressed than by such a scene.

There is an old adage—a barking dog never bites, which undoubtedly contains much truth, for it is hard to see how any dog could fasten its jaws around a nice juicy bite of leg, while, at the same time, emitting a prolonged and explosive bark. Many of us have taken consolation from this while the watch dogs heavy bay draws near as we speed towards safety, and yet, it seems to fail us in our hour of need, for suddenly the truth dawns upon us the dog may stop barking.

Dogs are perhaps the most expressive of all creatures. A dog can no more hide his feelings than he can hide his color, nor even as much so, for though his color may be disguised, his feelings cannot. His expression is not confined to his face as is that of humans, but the set of his ear, the waggle of his tail, and the very attitude of his whole body—all cry out to the world what *he* thinks about the matter.

Though there are as many types of dogs as there are stars in the heavens, and though these seem as different as day and night, they are all dogs, they can be nothing but dogs. They have about them the invisible and unseen mental attitude and expression, the incomprehensible and unsensible which binds them to each other and makes them all—just dogs.

RASSELE SWARTHOUT.

Top Row—Lewis, Lanum, Muir, Sprunger.
Bottom Row—Quickel, Deam, Lycan, Hays.

Athletic Board of Control

Officers

Chairman .... Mr. T. M. Deam
Secretary .... Helen Hays

Members 1922-1923

Paul Lewis
Franklin Lanum
Helen Hays
Lucille Quickle

Mr. Deam
Mr. Sprunger
Mr. Muir
Mrs. Lycan

FOOTBALL SQUAD, 1922

Top Row—Humiston, Austin, Pope, Adkins, Helphinstine, W. Johnson, White.
Second Row—Perry, Blowers, Barnard, Sattley, Richardson, Kile.
Third Row—Clark, Lehn, Sober, Theobald, O'Connell, Hill, Nicholson.
Bottom Row—G. Thompson, Johnson, Lanum, Lewis (Capt.), Briggs, D. Thompson, Arnold.

Football 1922

Although Decatur High held the small end of the scores of five out of eight games played, the games were all hard fought, and were rarely decided until the last half of the fourth quarter. The opponents in every case were stronger than those of past years and each team exhibited the highest class of football. From the financial standpoint the season was more successful than in past years, because of the good attendance at the games.

Under the leadership of Captain Lewis and the training of Coach Muir, the grid-warriors played many hard-fought games and upset the bucket by winning from the strong Mattoon eleven, who handed Urbana a trimming. The student body gave loyal support, many of them witnessing the Danville game in a downpour of rain.

The team suffered a serious blow in the first game when Howard Kile, the veteran tackle and ex-captain, suffered a broken leg.

The season of 1922 saw Kile, Captain Lewis, Adkins, Sober, Guy Thompson, Richardson, and McClelland play their last time for the red and white, but with the other seven lettermen under the leadership of captain-elect Helphinstine the season of 1923 promises to be successful. Much good material should be received from the second team and from Roosevelt and Central.

Football Scores

Decatur	0	Monticello	6
Decatur	7	Jacksonville	0
Decatur	13	Mattoon	3
Decatur	0	Urbana	45
Decatur	9	Peoria High	24
Decatur	(canceled)	Bloomington	(canceled)
Decatur	3	Danville	13
Decatur	17	Clinton	7
Decatur	3	Springfield	21

1922 Football Lettermen

Left End .... Don Thompson
Left Tackle .... Briggs, Perry
Left Guard .... Adkins
Center .... Helphinstine
Right Guard .... Guy Thompson, Lehn
Right Tackle .... Johnson, Kile
Left End .... McClelland
Quarterback .... Richardson
Left Halfback .... Lewis (Capt.)
Right Halfback .... Sober
Fullback .... Lanum

Do You Remember?

Ex-captain Kile, the housemoving tackle who uproots half the line.

Brigs, "Cupid" could stop them in the line or tear them up from "Briggs back" formation.

Adkins, the go-gettem guard who was always there. "Iceman" was always talking-it-up.

Helphinstine, the fighting center, who will lead them to victory in 1923. "Pate" was small, but mighty.

"Old" John Perry who played the game every minute and finally found his place at end.

Don Thompson, going down under a long pass from "Jake". His broad grin seems to say "Excuse mah dust, fellas".

"Russ" Lehn, "Bud" Johnson, Guy Thompson, and McClelland, "Mac". These fellows built up the stone wall in the line.

Our "rip 'em up" backfield. "Twisty" Richardson the "giant" quarter, Clare Sober the "Mercury-like" half, "Jake" Lanum, who beat all opponents in punting, passing and drop-kicking, was no slouch when it came to tackling and, last of all, Captain Lewis, "Lewy" the demon-like fighter and leader of his team.

Inter-Class Track

·For the first time in a good many years an inter-class track meet was held in the Decatur High School. The Seniors easily won the silver cup by piling up seventy-one points. The Juniors were second with fifty points and the Sophomores were third with twenty-two points. Richardson and Mc-Clelland were high point men for the Seniors, Hughes for the Juniors, and Brueck for the Sophomores.

SUMMARY OF EVENTS

50-yard dash—Richardson (Senior), first; Bennington (Junior), second; Hughes (Junior), third.

100-yard dash—Richardson (Senior), first; McClelland (Senior), second; Bennington (Junior), third.

220-yard dash—Richardson (Senior), first; Hughes (Junior), second; Bennington (Junior), third.

440-yard run—Hughes (Junior), first; Bear (Junior), second; Richardson (Senior), third.

880-yard run—Hughes (Junior), first; Bear (Junior), second; Cunningham (Senior), third.

One mile run—Cunningham (Senior), first; Bear (Junior), second; Austin (Senior), third.

Pole Vault—Barnard (Senior), first; McClelland (Senior), second; Baird (Junior), third.

Running Broad Jump—Richardson (Senior), first; Hughes (Junior), second; Brueck (Sophomore), third.

Discus Throw—Rothfuss (Senior), first; Brueck (Sophomore), second; Wilson (Sophomore), third.

Shot Put—Brueck (Sophomore), first; Rothfuss (Senior), second; McClelland (Senior), third.·

Javelin Throw—Brueck (Sophomore), first; McClelland (Senior), second; Baird (Junior), third.

200-yard low hurdles—McClelland (Senior), first; Bennington (Junior), second; Beaman (Sophomore), third.

High Jump—McClelland (Senior), first; Brueck (Sophomore), second; Danzeisen (Senior), third.

BASKETBALL, 1922-'23

Top Row—Sattley, Wilson, Muir (Coach), Rattan, Richardson.

Bottom Row—Mitchell, Perry (Capt.-elect), Lanum, Francis (Capt.), Offenstein, McGowan.

Basketball 1922-1923

Coming back strong in the latter half of their season after a pre-season slump the Decatur High School Basketball squad showed some real class and "nearly" copped the district Tourney. After finding "Jake" Lanum and Mitchell, Coach Muir developed a remarkable basket-ball machine. Our championship hopes were dashed to the ground by Maroa in the tournament, that team being the third team encountered in the tourney.

The special to Springfield was supported by two hundred students and all of the other games were well attended.

With Lanum, Offenstein, Sattley, McGowan, Perry, Mitchell and Wilson back and eligible to play, it is easy to predict a district champion and perhaps a state championship team for the 1923-1924 season.

Basketball Scores 1922-1923

December 16	Decatur........... 18	Tuscola 14
December 23	Decatur........... 21	Austin (Chi.)..... 25
January 5	Decatur........... 20	Monticello 23
January 12	Decatur........... 12	Clinton 27
January 13	Decatur........... 14	Urbana 28
January 19	Decatur........... 11	Springfield 29
January 26	Decatur........... 22	Danville 28
January 27	Decatur........... 29	Maroa 25
February 2	Decatur........... 31	University High... 25
February 3	Decatur........... 29	Mattoon 12
February 9	Decatur........... 21	Springfield 31
February 10	Decatur........... 27	Monticello 12
February 16	Decatur........... 16	Danville 15
February 23	Decatur........... 43	Clinton 9

TOURNAMENT

March 1	Decatur........... 27	Monticello 9
March 2	Decatur........... 22	Sullivan 11
March 3	Decatur........... 7	Maroa 9
Total	Decatur...........370	Opponents 332

Do You Remember?

The time John Perry made his field basket? They can't beat him at guard, however.

"Jake" Lanum's serene countenance as he dropped them all through the leather straps from the seventeen-foot line?

The interesting time that "Twisty" Richardson and "Bush" Sattley had in the final Clinton contest? A gentle game, was it not?

Fighting "Oakey" Offenstein the fellow who was never beaten?

Big easy going "Boliver", Captain Francis? He had a mean eye for the long baskets.

Virg McGowan? Emmett's kid brother?

Who said a sophomore couldn't play basketball?

Mitchell, the chubby guard from Central? A fit running mate for Perry.

"Bud" Rattan and Wilson always put up a good fight? The girls "oh!"

How good it felt to get revenge on Clinton, Monticello and Danville?

How we "nearly" whipped Austin High, last year's champions of Chicago?

Boys' Class Basketball

SENIORS
Murphy, Waggoner, Foltz, Hogle, Myers.

JUNIORS
Hughes, Smith, Stern, Leonard, Heffernan, Baird.

SOPHOMORES
Robbins, Niehaus, Miller, Greenwood, Ward.

G. A. A. OFFICERS
Top Row—Graham, Stewart, Morthland.
Bottom Row—McGurk, Lancaster (Pres.), Elliott.

The Girls' Athletic Association

The popularity of Girls' Athletics has noticeably increased during the past season. Although the facilities were limited, an opportunity was given all girls in the high school to participate in sports.

Tennis, one of the popular sports, was played in the early fall. Many exciting games were played, as the players were evenly matched. The results of the tournament are as follows:

First ....Mae Ross Taylor
Second ....Helen Hays
Third ....Charlotte Musser

One hundred girls came out to play the fascinating game of Hockey. There was keen competition for positions on all teams and much spirited rivalry between classes. The clash between the Juniors and Seniors was the strongest. The Seniors, with Lucille Quickle as captain, won the championship from Lucille Morthland's Juniors.

Much class spirit was shown among the teams in basketball. All teams were fast and showed excellent team-work. The sides were so evenly matched, it was necessary for the tournament to be played over.

In the G. A. A. meetings Mrs. Lycan helped the girls play for the various sports. Volley ball, baseball, swimming and hikes were taken up for the various spring activities.

G. A. A.

Officers

President ....MARGARET LANCASTER
Vice-President ....LUCILLE MORTHLAND
Secretary ....VIVIAN ELLIOTT
Treasurer ....PAULINE STEWART
Marshals ....CATHERINE GRAHAM, HELEN McGURK

Members 1922-1923

Dorothy Abaly
Annie Adams
Virginia Ammen
Lonnie Banta
Bernice Beckold
Rolande Brosseau
Helen Bunch
Martha Buxton
Edith Chapman
Elma Clayton
Helen Clayton
Helen Clements
Jennie Cochran
Catherine Coffey
Edna Cranston
Lillian Cook
Eloise Conaty
Grace Delaney
Bessie Denise
Guyneth Eaton
Vivian Elliott
Lillian Ellis
Lucille Erhart
Thelma Erickson
Edna Espy
Fern Faught
Goldie Fesler
Emily Fleck
Doris Fowler
Alice Fribourg
Mildred Foltz
Catherine Graham
Dorothy Hambright
Florence Hartman
Helen Hays
Shirley Hays
Josephine Higman
Nancy Hill

Zella Himstedt
Marjorie Hodgins
Martha Holt
Helen Johns
Emily Johnson
Doris Kelley
Velma Keilman
Margaret Lancaster
Edith Landers
Virginia Lipscomb
Lina Lindsay
Minnie Lunsford
Grace March
Nelius Martin
Eleanor Marshall
Helen McGurk
Jane McKenzie
Ada Mae Merris
Mary E. Michels
Cora M. Michener
Anna Louise Mills
Mary Jane Mills
Nellie Morarity
Lucille Morthland
Charlotte Musser
Pauline Nolan
Eleanor Ott
Geraldine Owen
Della Peterson
Helen Phillips
Jane Pluck
Lucille Quickel
Ara Rawlings
Helen Rives
Helen Russell
Celia Rosen
Lucille Schudel

Florence Scott
Eleanor Shaw
Dorothy Shaw
Roberta Shields
Roma Shoemaker
Pauline Stewart
Dorothy Stuckey
Mildred Stoutenborough
Elizabeth Tait
Mae Ross Taylor
Anna Tauber
Helen Tucker
Ruth Vance
Frances Webb
Ruth Wicklein
Frances Hines
Jestin McKelvey
Gertrude Gustin
Margaret Watkins
Louise Mason
Lois Boyd
Anna Higgins
Nellie Weber
Jola Brundage
Helen Moffett
Esther Peterson
Mary K. McDonald
Helen Voorhies
Julia Bohon
Ruby Wikoff
Frances Flint
Ruth Reedy
Luella Marshall
Ruth Stubbs
Maxine Trimble
Margaret Kistler
Dorothea Bobb

Girls' Class Basketball

SENIORS
Lycan (Coach), Graham, Hays, Shields, Kelley, Clements, Conaty, Busch, Lancaster, Quickel.

JUNIORS
Lycan (Coach), Marshall, Morthland, Hartman, Higman, Fleck, Tait, Phillips, Banta, Musser.

SOPHOMORES
Lycan (Coach), Shoemaker, Schudel, Byers, Brundage, Foltz, Kielman, Lindsay, Ammen, Vance, Maffit.

Girls' Hockey Teams

Top Row—Tohill, Faught, Lindsay, Foltz, Fribourg, E. Clayton, Mills, Ammen, Vance.
Second Row—Owens, Hartman, Erickson, Tucker, Himstead, Schudel, Kielman, M. J. Mills, Elliott.
Third Row—Higman, McGurk, Fowler, Hugenberger, Phillips, Morthland, Ellis, Delaney, Hodgins, Fleck.
Fourth Row—Clements, Martin, Hays, Conaty, Cranston, Hines, Stuckey, Pluck.
Bottom Row—Hambright, Shaw, Ryman, Shields, Clayton, Quickel, Lancaster, Michener, Graham, Kelley.

SOCIETIES

Standing—James A. Rattan (Pres.).
First Row—Rowdybush, Sullivan, Briggs.
Second Row—B. Holt, E. Hartmann, Yoder, Elliott.
Third Row—Gollings, Offenstein, Hays, Schaub.
Fourth Row—Foltz, F. Hartman, Hostetler, Sprunger.

Student Council

Officers

President ....James Rattan
Vice-President ....Florence Hartman
Secretary ......:....Marjorie Sullivan, Bettie Holt

Members 1922-1923

Seniors	Juniors	Sophomores
Lester Foltz	Florence Hartman	Vivian Elliott
Elizabeth Hartmann	Paul Offenstein	Shirley Hayes
Bettie Holt	Charles Schaub	Frank Gollings
Margaret Humphrey	Marjorie Sullivan	Frank Rowdybush
James Rattan	Roger Yoder	Sterling Briggs

Top Row—Wicklein, Davidson, Tucker, Wagenseller, Milnes, Foulke, Denz, Powers, Wood.
Second Row—D. Shaw, McGurk, Widick, Erickson, Bopp, Skinner, Cline, King, Harris.
Third Row—Fesler, Barnett, Kincaid, Dearth, Pease, Melton, Krumsick, E. Shaw.
Bottom Row—Benton, Waltz, Bruner, Sloan; Shields, Rives, Anderson, Hill, Walden.

Aristos

Officers

	First Semester	Second Semester
President	ZOLA SLOAN	MARGARET HUMPHREY
Vice-President	CONSTANCE WALTZ	ROBERTA SHIELDS
Secretary	MAURINE EVANS	MIRIAM BRUNER
Treasurer	VIOLA MELTON	VIOLA MELTON
English Critic	RUTH ACKERMAN	RUTH ACKERMAN
Parliamentarian	ROBERTA SHIELDS	DOROTHY SHAW
Marshal	ELEANOR WOOD	FANNY POWERS
Marshal	DOROTHY DAVIDSON	LOUISE DENZ

Members 1922-1923

Ruth Ackerman
Grace Anderson
Esther Barnett
Charlotte Benton
Mabel Bledsoe
Louise Bopp
Miriam Bruner
Lockie Cline
Dorothy Davidson
Dorothy Dirth
Louise Denz
Irma Dunn
Thelma Ericson
Edna Espy
Maurine Evans

Harriett Foulke
Helen Harris
Margaret Humphrey
Jessie King
Angeline Kincaid
Helen Krumsiek
Nancy Hill
Anna Hines
Helen McGurk
Viola Melton
Louise Milnes
Eleanor Pease
Helen Rives
Helen Rucker
Goldie Fesler

Margaret Rives
Dorothy Shaw
Eleanor Shaw
Roberta Shields
Helen Skinner
Zola Sloan
Bertha Shoemaker
Constance Waltz
Janice Widick
Katherine Wagenseller
Ruth Walden
Ruth Wicklein
Eleanor Wood
Fanny Powers

Top Row—Pritchett, Steiner, Witt, Clark, Pollard, Williams.
Second Row—Parrish, Starr, Rosenberg, Winters, Wait.
Third Row—Henderson, Goodwin, Miller, Danzeisen, Pitner, Heil.
Bottom Row—Pope, Witzeman (Pres.), Nordman (Advisor), Rothfuss, Yoder.

Rotaro

Officers

	First Semester	Second Semester
President	W. Junior Rothfuss	Everett Witzeman
Vice-President	Everett Witzeman	Jack Henderson
Secretary	Carl Goodwin	Herman Pritchett
Treasurer	Eugene Danzeisen	Eugene Danzeisen
Sergeants-at-Arms	{ Lawrence Witt, Frank English }	{ W. Junior Rothfuss, William Pitner }
Parliamentarian	Jack Henderson	Roger Yoder
English Critic	Herman Pritchett	John Heil

Members 1922-1923

Eugene Danzeisen	Harry Miller	Franklin Wait
Frank English	Lealdes Eaton	Tom Clark
Jack Henderson	Chester Walker	Thomas Pope
Wayne Parrish	Lawrence Witt	Wallace Tait
Ned Pollard	Roger Yoder	Allen Jones
Herman Pritchett	Joe Rosenberg	Wilfred Steiner
W. Junior Rothfuss	Tom Bohon	Williard Williams
Everett Witzeman	William Pitner	Nathan Haines
Carl Goodwin	Eric Winter	Charles Fishback
William Storr	John Heil	Everett Wilson

Top Row—Scott, Kelley, Lancaster, Busch, Conley, Abel.
Second Row—Hays, Graham, Watkins, Wells, Hardbarger, Coles, Drennan.
Third Row—Rhodes, Hugenberger, Friend, Chaille, Saling, Adams.
Bottom Row—Denise, Mason, Stewart, Hartmann (Pres.), Burke, Hambright, Martin.

Agora

Officers

	First Semester	Second Semester
President	DOROTHY WILSON	ELIZABETH HARTMANN
Vice-President	ELIZABETH HARTMANN	BONNIE REGAN
Secretary	DOROTHY HAMBRIGHT	PAULINE STEWART
Treasurer	MILDRED BURKE	MILDRED BURKE
English Critic	BONNIE REGAN	ERMINA BUSCH
English Critic	HELEN CLAYTON	LOUISE MASON
Parliamentarian	FLORENCE COLES	DOROTHY HAMBRIGHT
Marshal	CORA MICHENER	NELIUS MARTIN
Marshal	CATHERINE GRAHAM	MARGARET LANCASTER
Press Reporter	ERMINA BUSCH	

Members 1922-1923

Muriel Abell
Annie Adams
Ermina Busch
Helen Clayton
Florence Coles
Auline Conley
Bessie Denise
Dorothy Drennan
Catherine Graham
Dorothy Hambright
Helen Hayes
Elizabeth Hartmann

Lois Hardbarger
Reba Hugenberger
Velma Keilman
Doris Kelly
Hazel Leathers
Nelius Martin
Inez McElrath
Bonnie Regan
Celia Rosen
Pauline Stewart
Florence Scott
Angeline Saling

Mae Ross Taylor
Dorothy Wilson
Margaret Watkins
Mildred Burke
Louise Mason
Bernice Beckold
Thyra Friend
Alice Wells
Loreen Rhodes
Mable Kiester
Margaret Lancaster
Lucille Chaille

Top Row—Walsh, Carr, Hansen, Rubenstein, Talbott, Bear.
Second Row—Dougherty, Lutz, Crain, Gulick, Cunningham, Diller, Coles.
Third Row—Chapman, Hastings, Eckert, Dickinson, Karr, Gollings.
Bottom Row—Austin, Pease, Hubbart (Advisor), Lupton (Pres.), Swarthout, Turner, Abrams.

Forum

Officers

	First Period	Second Period	Third Period
President	WILLIARD HANSEN	PERLEY LUPTON	PERLEY LUPTON
Vice-President	WILLIS DOUGHERTY	MATHIAS ECKERT	FRANK ROWDYBUSCH
Secretary	LEMENT RUCKER	BENJAMIN HASTINGS	WILLIS DOUGHERTY
Treasurer	FRANK GULICK	FRANK GULICK	FRANK GULICK
Parliamentarian	HERBERT AUSTIN	WILLIARD HANSEN	BENJAMIN HASTINGS

Members 1922-1923

Herbert Austin	Rollin Pease	Keith Talbott
Franklin Bear	Meyer Rubinstein	Eugene Abrams
Alan Chapman	Rassele Swarthout	Frank Gollings
Harry Coles	Perley Lupton	Dale Karr
Willis Dougherty	Mathias Eckert	Maurice Crain
Arthur Gleason	Roy Kashner	Nathan Carr
Frank Gulick	Frank Rowdybusch	Jack Eisele
Willard Hansen	Daniel Lutz	James Turner
Benjamin Hastings	Lee Dickinson	Walter Diller

Top Row—Higgins, Voorhies, Koscielny, Mooney, Stanjey, Trimble.
Second Row—Suleeba, Bohon, Chamberlain, Buxton, Drennan, Ross.
Third Row—Pollard, Duggan, Foran, Lindsay, Schudel, Hackett.
Bottom Row—Dunn, McDonald, Guest (Pres.), Pease, Ammen, Phillips.

Arion

Officers

	First Semester	Second Semester
President	INEZ McELRATH	NANETTE GUEST
Vice-President	MAE ROSS TAYLOR	MARION PEASE
Secretary	NANETTE GUEST	VIRGINIA AMMEN
Treasurer	LOUISE BOPP	MARY K. McDONALD
English Critic	MARY K. McDONALD	IRIS MOONEY
Parliamentarian	VIRGINIA AMMEN	JULIA BOHON
Marshal	MARTHA BUXTON	MARY HACKETT
Marshal	LINA LINDSEY	MAXINE TRIMBLE

Members 1922-1923

Virginia Ammen
Julia Bohon
Ellna Clayton
Lucille Chamberlain
Margaret Duggan
Martha Buxton
Melba Dunn
Mildred Foltz
Nanette Guest
Mary Hackett
Anna Higgins

Agnes Kascielny
Lina Lindsey
Mary K. McDonald
Evelyn Milligan
Iris Mooney
Marion Pease
Leone Phillips
Virginia Pié
Gladys Pollard
Ruth Ross
Olga Schiwek

Marion Suleeba
Lucile Schudel
Muriel Stanley
Maxine Trimble
Helen Voorhies
Carolyn Drennan
Loretta Foran
Elizabeth Hinton
Doris Hulett

Top Row—Thomas, Nordman, Bear, Hubbart.
Bottom Row—Busch, Danzeisen, McClelland, Humphrey.

Public Speaking Board of Control

Officers

Chairman ....EUGENE DANZEISEN
Secretary ....ERMINA BUSCH

Members 1922-1923

Ermina Busch   Miss Thomas
Eugene Danzeisen   Mr. Nordman
Glenn McClelland   Miss Bear
Margaret Humphrey   Mr. Hubbart

Top Row—Wilson, Clark, Pritchett.
Second Row—Jones, Swarthout, Winters, Lupton.
Bottom Row—Sloan, Hubbart (Coach), Nordman (Coach), Pollock.

Debate

First Semester	*Second Semester*
Perley Lupton	Vivian Pollock
Herman Pritchett	Everett Wilson
Allen Jones	Herman Pritchett
Zola Sloan	Zola Sloan
Eric Winters	Eric Winters
Rassele Swarthout	Perley Lupton
Jessie Glasgow }—Alternates	Tom Clark }—Alternates
Joe Rosenberg	Florence Coles

Top Row—Saling, Milnes, Sloan, Foulke, Braden, Benton, Virden.
Second Row—Garmen, Bone, Hostetler (Advisor), Dittus, Grothe, Glasgow, Simons.
Third Row—Dearth, Denise, Barnett, Hugenberger, Cannon, Salogga, Pease.
Bottom Row—Veech, Cline, Benton, Sutton, Wagenseller, Harris.

Ethical Club

Officers

President .... ELIZABETH HARTMANN
Vice-President .... VERNA SUTTON
Treasurer .... RUTH GROTHE
Secretary .... LOUISE MILNES
English Critic .... KATHERINE WAGENSELLER
Parliamentarian .... ZOLA SLOAN

Members 1922-1923

Freda Barnett
Bernice Beckhold
Charlotte Benton
Marian Benton
Velma Bone
Netha Braden
Miriam Bruner
Gertrude Cannon
Lockie Cline
Dorothy Dearth
Eleanor Dittis
Harriet Foulke
Ferne Garman

Jessie Glasgow
Ruth Grothe
Phyllis Hams
Lela Harris
Reba Hugenberger
Vera Kater
Viola Melton
Louise Milnes
Eleanor Pease
Angeline Saling
Zola Sloan
Freda Salogga

Verna Sutton
Dorma Veach
Hazel Virden
Katherine Wagenseller
Bessie Denise
Alta Bain
Beatrice Vick
Ruth Ross
Carolyn Drennan
Elizabeth Hartmann
Dorothy Kitchen
Ruth Cratz

Top Row—Wilson, Clark, Pritchett.
Second Row—Jones, Swarthout, Winters, Lupton.
Bottom Row—Sloan, Hubbart (Coach), Nordman (Coach), Pollock.

Debate

First Semester

Perley Lupton
Herman Pritchett
Allen Jones
Zola Sloan
Eric Winters
Rassele Swarthout
Jessie Glasgow }—Alternates
Joe Rosenberg

Second Semester

Vivian Pollock
Everett Wilson
Herman Pritchett
Zola Sloan
Eric·Winters
Perley Lupton
Tom Clark }—Alternates
Florence Coles

Top Row—Saling, Milnes, Sloan, Foulke, Braden, Benton, Virden.
Second Row—Garmen, Bone, Hostetler (Advisor), Dittus, Grothe, Glasgow, Simons.
Third Row—Dearth, Denise, Barnett, Hugenberger, Cannon, Salogga, Pease.
Bottom Row—Veech, Cline, Benton, Sutton, Wagenseller, Harris.

Ethical Club

Officers

President ....ELIZABETH HARTMANN
Vice-President ....VERNA SUTTON
Treasurer ....RUTH GROTHE
Secretary ....LOUISE MILNES
English Critic ....KATHERINE WAGENSELLER
Parliamentarian ....ZOLA SLOAN

Members 1922-1923

Freda Barnett	Jessie Glasgow	Verna Sutton
Bernice Beckhold	Ruth Grothe	Dorma Veach
Charlotte Benton	Phyllis Hams	Hazel Virden
Marian Benton	Lela Harris	Katherine Wagenseller
Velma Bone	Reba Hugenberger	Bessie Denise
Netha Braden	Vera Kater	Alta Bain
Miriam Bruner	Viola Melton	Beatrice Vick
Gertrude Cannon	Louise Milnes	Ruth Ross
Lockie Cline	Eleanor Pease	Carolyn Drennan
Dorothy Dearth	Angeline Saling	Elizabeth Hartmann
Eleanor Dittis	Zola Sloan	Dorothy Kitchen
Harriet Foulke	Freda Salogga	Ruth Cratz
Ferne Garman		

Top Row—Helphinstine, Gulick.
Bottom Row—Offenstein, Sober, O'Connell.

Juniors

Officers

President ....CLARE SOBER
Vice-President ....TOM O'CONNELL
Secretary ....PAUL OFFENSTEIN
Treasurer ....PAYTON HELPHINSTINE
Sergeants-at-Arms.....FRANK GULICK, RUSSELL LEHN

Junior Committees

Social

Thomas O'Connell (Chairman)
Virginia Lipscomb
Roger Yoder
Franklin Bear
Martha Holt

Floral and Decoration

Lois Boyd (Chairman)
Alonzella Banta
Frank Gulick
Charles Schaub

Athletic

Arthur Gleason (Chairman)
Florence Hartman
Thelma Erickson
Frank Mahan

Top Row—Kistler, Harpold, Wright, Rosenthal, Sleeter, Shelton, Donavan, Filson, Conaty, Hill.
Second Row—Dunn, Orey, E. Shaw, Adams, Rosen, Myers, Simonds, Phillips, Harris, Martin, Lancaster, Hockaday.
Third Row—Peel, McCarter, Michener, Sanders, Higgins, McKenzie, Saling, Hodgins, D. Shaw, Peters, Ray.
Bottom Row—Wasson, R. Shields, G. Shields, Landers, Ricketts, McGurk, Wells, Dillinger, McRay, Boyer.

Girls' Glee Club

Officers

	First Semester	Second Semester
President	ROBERTA SHIELDS	MILDRED RICKETTS
Vice-President	MILDRED RICKETTS	DOROTHY BOYER
Secretary	DOROTHY BOYER	HELEN PHILLIPS
Treasurer	MILDRED SIMONDS	MILDRED SIMONDS
Librarian	MARGARET KISTLER	MILDRED HILL
Pianist	MARGARET KISTLER	MARGARET KISTLER
Press Reporter	HELEN ROSENTHAL	ELENOR SHAW

Members 1922-1923

First Soprano—
Ethel Adams
Dorothy Boyer
Freeda Burnett
Nancy Hill
Blanch McCarter
Rena Landers
Nellie Orey
Grace Raffe
Roberta Shields
Eleanor Shaw
Ruby Wassen
Goldie Ray
Eleanor Peters
Mary Donovan
Helen Clayton

First Soprano—
Angeline Saling
Gertrude Gustin
Grace Shields

Second Soprano—
Dorothy Filson
Dorothy Shaw
Mildred Simmonds
Ruth Shelton
Freda Sanders
Elizabeth Wright
Helen Henebery
Mildred Dunn
Helen Phillips
Nelius Martin
Ruth Meyers

Alto—
Marjorie Hodgins
Anna Higgins
Mildred McCrory
Helen Rosenthal
Mildred Ricketts
Dorothy Sleeter
Helen Harris
Celia Rosen
Helen McGurk
Margaret Lancaster
Minnie Brubeck
Helen Harpold
Mildred Wells
Norma Peel
Eloise Conaty

Top Row—Eckert, Van Bellehem, Witzeman, Foran, Wilson, C. Jenkins.
Second Row—Fenton, Hastings, Newlin, Litterst, Pollard, Rader, Rubenstein.
Third Row—Cain, Lathrop, Nicholson, Munch, Leonard, Lonnon.
Bottom Row—D. Jenkins, Stough, Cunningham, Sayre, Walker (Pres.), Blickle, Henninger.

Boys' Glee Club

Officers

President ....Chester Walker
Vice-President ....Ted Brown
Treasurer ....Ray Newlin

Members 1922-1923

First Tenor—
Chester Walker
Everett Biddle
Ted Brown
Raymond Lannon
Kenneth Henninger
David Jenkins
Carol Jenkins
Mathias Eckert

Second Tenor—
Benjamin Hastings
John Stough
Ralph Lathrop
Meyer Rubinstein

First Bass—
Maurice Crain
Guy Litterst

First Bass—
William Nicholson
Davis Wilson
Ray Blickle
Ray Sayre
James Van Bellehem

Second Bass—
Everett Witzeman
Ray Newlin
Eugene Foran
Thorton Rader
Walter Cunningham
Ned Pollard
Lawrence Leonard
William Fenton

Accompanist—
Foster Brashear

Top Row—Olive, Scranton, Hackett, Hastings, Ackerman, Turner, Hansen.
Second Row—Leathers, Hugenberger, Denise, Milnes, Coles, Melton, Foulke, Walden.
Third Row—Pollock, Scurlock, Busch, Hartmann, Harkness, Shields, Harris, Romanus.
Bottom Row—Newlin, Danzeisen, Lupton, Sloan (Ed.-in-chief), Bohon, Brady, Nicholson, Goodwin.

The Observer Staff

Editor-in-Chief	ZOLA SLOAN
Business Manager	TOM BOHON
Advertising Manager	FLOYD WYKOFF / PERLEY LUPTON
Assistant Business Manager	WILLIAM NICHOLSON
Assistant Advertising Manager	EUGENE DANZEISEN
Assistant Editor	ROY BRADY
Local Editors	FLORENCE COLES / RUTH ACKERMAN / WILLIARD HANSEN
Societies Editors	RUTH WALDEN / CARL GOODWIN
Alumni Editor	ELIZABETH HARTMANN
Exchange Editors	ERMINA BUSCH / VIVIAN POLLOCK
Athletic Editors	PAUL OFFENSTEIN / ROBERTA SHIELDS
Joke Editors	MARGARET ROMANUS / JAMES TURNER
Cartoonist	LESTER FOLTZ
Art Editors	HELEN HACKETT / CATHERINE SCURLOCK

Top Row—Orey, Rawlings, Moore, Shoemaker, Sanders.
Second Row—Burnett, Adams, Olive, Cummings, Michener, Lunsford.
Third Row—Zeff, Constant, Hines, Dunaway, Parker (Advisor), Rosenthal, Thomas.
Bottom Row—Lester, Bruner, Foran, Goodwin (Pres.), Yoder.

Commercial Club

Officers

	First Semester	Second Semester
President	ROGER YODER	CARL GOODWIN
Vice-President	CORA MICHENER	CORA MICHENER
Secretary	HELEN HARPOLD	FREDA SANDERS
Treasurer	NELLIE OREY	NELLIE OREY

Members 1922-1923

Ethel Adams
Anna May Bauer
Dorothy Barnhart
Ruth Beck
Ruth Burnette
Miriam Bruner
Alberta Constant
Grace Cummings
Lois Dunaway
Dorothy Ehrhart
Carl Goodwin
Anna Hines

Minnie Lunsford
Retha Merris
Cora Michener
Sarah Moore
Jeston McKelvey
Freda Olive
Nellie Orey
Helen Russell
Helen Rosenthal
Ara Rawlings
Freda Sanders

Bertha Shumaker
Herbert Theobald
Alberta Zeff
Beatrice Vick
Lorraine Lester
Eugene Foran
Rosella Thomas
Muriel Abell
Clarence Allbright
Helen Harpold
Roger Yoder

Top Row—Dillinger, Bone, Sutton, Simons, Logan.
Second Row—Rosen, Troutman, Deck, Milnes, Salogga.
Third Row—Zeff, Foale, Karr, Sloan, Foulke, Coles.
Bottom Row—Lively, Kincaid, Hardbarger, Heil (Pres.), Chaille, Saling.

Social Science Club

Officers

	First Semester	Second Semester
President	FLORENCE COLES	JOHN HEIL
Vice-President	ZOLA SLOAN	LOIS HARDBARGER
Secretary	CHARLOTTE BENTON	LUCILLE CHAILLE
Treasurer	JOE ROSENBERG	JOE ROSENBERG
Parliamentarian	RUTH WALDEN	ROBERTA SHIELDS
English Critic	LUCILLE CHAILLE	ZOLA SLOAN
Marshal	EVERETT BIGGERS	ANGELINE SALING
Marshal	ELEANOR MARSHALL	ANGELINE KINCAID
Press Reporter	ANGELINE SALING	HARRIET FOULKE
Observer Reporter	LOUISE MILNES	LOUISE MILNES

Members 1922-1923

Bernice Beckold
Lucille Chaille
Florence Coles
Bernice Dillinger
Harriet Foulke
Lois Hardbarger
Dale Karr
Angeline Kincaid
Selma Lively

Louise Milnes
Celia Rosen
Joe Rosenberg
Angeline Saling
Zola Sloan
Verna Sutton
Bernice Troutman
Inez McElrath
John Heil

Roberta Shields
Charles Deck
John Foale
Mae Simmonds
Grace Cummings
Freda Salogga
Alberta Zeff
Velma Bone

Top Row—Pollard, Slink, Walker, Wykoff, Newlin, Blickle.
Middle Row—Pygman, Connard, Bradley, Singer, Myers, Pope, Evans, Witzeman.
Bottom Row—Berry, Durham, Kashner, Harkness, Steiner, Tommasi, Briggs, Walters, Witt, Davis.

Band

Officers

President .... CHESTER WALKER
Vice-President .... LESLIE HARKNESS
Secretary .... LEALDES EATON
Treasurer .... FLOYD WYKOFF

Members 1922-1923

Solo Cornets—
Rollin Pease
Leslie Harkness
Roy Kashner

First Cornets—
Kenneth Durham
Donald Pygman

Second Cornet—
John Connard

Solo Clarinet—
Robert Walters

First Clarinet—
Lawrence Witt

Second Clarinet—
Everett Witzeman

Third Clarinet—
Lyman Davis

C Saxaphones—
Bennett Bradley
Everett Evans

Eb Saxaphones—
George Singer
Lealdes Eaton
Thomas Pope

Baritone—
Richard Shirk
Earl Ramsey

Bass—
Ned Pollard

Alto Horn—
Lorenzo Shaffer

First Horn—
Ray Newlin

Trombones—
Chester Walker
Floyd Wykoff

Drums—
Sterling Briggs
Robert Beary

Orchestra

*Director—*JOSEPH TOMMASI

Members 1922-1923

First Violins—
Robert Walters
Maynard Lipe
Dorothy Glosser
Helen Hockaday
William Sawyer
Wayne Edie
Alice Weld
Helen Scurlock
Lynn Bunch
Alline Brockett

Second Violins—
Everett Biggers
Arline Conely
Reba Hugenberger
Ned Pollard
Maxwell Pygman

Second Violins—
Wilfred Steiner
Ruth Wicklein
Floy Keister

Viola—
Lorine Rhodes

Cello—
Raymond Blickle

Clarinets—
Lawrence Witt
Everett Witzeman

C Saxaphones—
Bennett Bradley
Daniel Lutz

Eb Saxaphone—
George Singer

Cornets—
Rollin Pease
Leslie Harkness
Donald Pygman
John Connard

Trombones—
Chester Walker
Clifford Mitchell

Horn—
Ray Newlin

Alto Horn—
Lorenzo Shaffer

Drums—
Sterling Briggs

Piano—
Henrietta Clark

Top Row—Baker, Edgecombe, White, Gulick, Kennedy, Sutterer.
Second Row—Brown, Turk, Richardson, Beaman, Garver, Roney.
Third Row—Rowland, Stare, Davis, McCracken, Cullum, Hastings, Maxon.
Bottom Row—Cannon, Scranton, Dial, Hammond (Advisor), Robbins, Morthland, Hopkins.

Agriculture Club

Officers

President ....MATHIAS ECKERT
Vice-President ....TED BROWN
Secretary ....EVERETT EVANS
Treasurer ....BARNER TROUTMAN

Members 1922-1923

Jack Earl	Robert Robbins	William Todare
Lyman Davis	Walter Seegar	Donald Stare
Jay Shutter	DeLong Kennedy	Walter Cullum
Harold Edgecombe	Frank Gulick	Norman Scranton
Stuart Baker	Lawrence Leonard	Thurman Dial
Earnest Rowland	August Peverly	Eugene White
Glenn Richdish	Merton Garver	Kenneth Keown
John Hopkins	Oscar Caay	Mathias Eckert
Lesley Turk	Edwin Beaman	Ted Brown
Arthur Gleason	Dale Barnett	Everett Evans
Benjamin Hastings	Chester Cann	Barner Troutman

Junior Art League

Officers

President ....Clairbelle Fisk
Vice-President ....Frances Sellers
Secretary ....Esther Scranton
Treasurer ....Edna Quickel
Marshal ....Wallace Hogle
English Critic ....Anna Walker

Members 1922-1923

Rolando Brosseau   Frances Sellers
Martha Hawkins   Esther Scranton
Jeannette Powell   Edna Quickel
Jessie Glasgow   Wallace Hogle
Ruby Wasson   Anna Walker
Clairbelle Fisk

Poster Club

Officers

President ....Esther Scranton
Vice-President ....Edna Quickel
Secretary ....Janice Widick
Treasurer ....Wallace Hogle
English Critic ....Helen Hackett

Members 1922-1923

Rolando Brosseau   Jane Pluck
Alice Colvin   Edna Quickle
Clairbelle Fisk   Esther Scranton
Jessie Glasgow   Francis Sellars
Helen Hackett   Pauline Stewart
Wallace Holge   Ruby Wasson
Glen Morris   Janice Widick

FUNCTIONS

Top Row—Sullivan, Evans.
Bottom Row—Folkers, Holt.

The Review Story Contest

The twenty-seventh annual Review Story Contest was the most success-ful ever held. The contest this year broke all previous records in the num-ber of stories entered, one hundred and seventy-four having been submitted. The prizes were won by two seniors and two juniors. The first prize was awarded Miss Bettie Holt; second, Miss Marjorie Sullivan; third, Karl Kolkers and fourth, Miss Maurine Evans.

Simplicity and a sense of humor distinguished the prize stories. Good English, rather than interesting stories, was given first consideration. Gen-erally speaking, it was a good class of entries. Originality made many of the stories unusually interesting.

Those who have won prizes and honor-distinction have reason to be proud of their achievement. The judges for the contest were, Mrs. Cora B. Ryman, County Superintendent of Schools, Robert I. Hunt and Mrs. Lindley Huff.

Senior Party

The senior party was an eminent success. The "gym" was never more cleverly nor more originally decorated than it was on Saturday night, December 10. Southern moss was draped around the balcony, and blue and silver ribbons of paper reached from one side to the other. At the east end of the gymnasium was a large emblem, 1923, arranged in the class colors, blue and silver. A light was reflected upon it so that it was the most conspicuous spot in the room.

At eight o'clock there was a grand march led by Glenn McClelland, the class president, and Miss Dorothy Wilson, vice-president.

William Pitner read the class prophecy which was written by Herman Pritchett, Jack Henderson and himself.

While refreshments were served, Mr. Homebrook played popular music. Homebrook's five-piece orchestra played for the dancing.

The senior advisors and the class patrons were chaperons.

Junior Party

Two hundred members of the class of 1924 enjoyed their first class party which was held Saturday night, November the eleventh, in the high school gymnasium. Fifty patrons and patronesses as well as the class advisors were present. A very delightful program was given between the dances. The class prophecy, written by Florence Hartmann and Josephine Higman drew forth many laughs from the members of the class who saw themselves as they were to be fifty years hence. A dance by Ilda Koronko and Cecile Jack, and a vocal solo by Margaret Kistler pleased the juniors and their guests.

The walls of the gymnasium were draped with American flags, the ceiling was covered with a net-work of red, white and blue streamers, in keeping with Armistice Day. At both ends of the gym and over the baskets were arranged the class colors of orange and blue. Refreshments of frappe and wafers were served during the evening. Yeagle's orchestra furnished the music for the dancing.

Junior-Senior Reception

The annual Junior-Senior Reception held on the evening of April the twenty-eighth was the most beautiful party ever held in the gymnasium. The big room was marvelously decorated, following the King Tut-ankh-Amen style. The ceiling and walls of the gym were hidden by long streamers of Egyptian paper in soft tones of lavendar, brown, pink, blue, tan, and green which made the bare gym into a colorful and charming palace. Wide bands of paper with Egyptian figures in silhouette constituted a border around the upper part of the walls and from the center of the room hund a large square lamp with the silhouette figures on the four sides.

At one end of the room was placed a replica of the Senior shield, finished in gold, and placed on a black background. At the other end was the sepulchre of King Tut which was broken open during the evening revealing Dorothy Abaly, wrapped in many windings to imitate a mummy. Rising slowly to her full height, she danced out on the floor, unwinding her wrappings as she danced. As part of the entertainment Bennett Bradley played a saxophone solo, and Virginia Lipscomb read the prophecy. Most of the evening was spent in dancing, Lee Homebrook's orchestra furnishing the music.

Entrance to the gym was gained through the corridor which was filled with lounging chairs, couches, tall shaded lamps, beautiful rugs and ferns. The stairs leading from the corridor to the gym was darkened by the use of dull gray paper in imitation of the entrance to the king's tomb. Emerging from the dim entrance, the color and beauty burst forth on the sight of the guests as did the treasure room of old King Tut on the sight of Lord Carnarvon.

The receiving line was at the entrance of the gym. It consisted of the Junior Class officers, their friends, and the head of the Junior advisors, Miss Hull. The grand march was led by Clare Sober, President of the Junior Class, and Miss Bettie Holt. Patrons and patronesses were the parents of students and some members of the faculty were also present.

The Sophomore Party

The Sophomores were given a delightful entertainment in the form of a Hallowe'en masquerade party. The gymnasium was decorated with black cats, witches and corn stalks. At one end of the gymnasium a fire place had been built where a very realistic fire burned merrily.

A Grand March started the entertainment. Immediately following the sophs were amused by a Harold Lloyd comedy. Following the comedy there was a piano solo and then a dance by the witches.

Refreshments were served very cleverly. The doughnuts were passed on long sticks, then every one was given an apple. The rest of the time was spent in dancing.

The Forum-Rotaro Party

The Forum-Rotaro party, held on the evening of December 22, was one of the most pleasing social events of the year. Besides the regular members present, the alumni of both societies were invited, and many of them attended. Among those present were Paul Evans, Robert Taylor, John Ditto, Frank Sheffler, J. B. Austin and Corwin Lewis who are now students at Millikin University; Herbert B. Lowe, Philip Bruso, Clarence Ray and Henry Heil now attending the University of Illinois; Clifford McKelvey of Wabash University, Robert J. Wood of Philips Andover, Douglas Johnson of St. John's Military Academy, Royal McClelland and David Dresback who are not attending school at the present time.

The decorations were in keeping with the Yuletide season. Red and green streamers extended from a great Christmas tree, which stood in the center of the floor, to the walls. The tree was covered with bright colored ornaments, icicles, and snow.

Dancing was the feature of the evening. Bennett Bradley delighted the guests with a saxophone solo. Refreshments of grape punch and cakes were served. Virgil Byers' orchestra played for the dancing.

Athletic Party

The same color scheme was carried out in the Athletic dance that was used in the Girls' Athletic Association affair. The red and white ribbons of paper were draped from each side of the balcony. The large trophy blankets which the boys on the different athletic teams use, helped in decorating the main floor.

The party was held on Friday night, February 24. The guests danced from eight to eleven o'clock. Robert Caldwell's orchestra furnished the music.

G. A. A. Party

The Girls' Athletic Association had their yearly function on Friday night, January 26; it was given in the form of a dance.

The gymnasium was decorated with the high school colors. Red and white ribbons of paper were draped from one side of the balcony to the other, making a lattice effect. There was a triangle on the lattice at the farthest end of the room and Marion's Novelette Orchestra was placed behind it.

The refreshments were pineapple ice with a red cherry and cookies, which also completed the color scheme.

Agora-Aristos Banquet

On November 17, Agora and Aristos joined to have their social function of the semester. This banquet was attended by seventy girls with their guests, who were all ready to begin the good time at 6:30 o'clock. The color scheme was orange and green. Sweetheart roses were placed in the center of the table; green ribbons were tied at one end to the roses, at the other to the hand-painted place cards and programs.

Margaret Humphrey was the toast mistress. The program was started by Dorothy Wilson, president of Agora, and Zola Sloan, president of Aristos. Marjorie Sullivan and Dorothy Hambright each gave a reading. Mrs. Hostetler gave "A Message" to the girls. Mr. Deam and Mr. Richeson spoke on the value of literary societies, Miss Yoder on "Programs," Mrs. Nelson gave a short talk.

The girls then went to the auditorium to see "The Florist Shop" and "The Silver Thread" which were given by the E. A. Gastman School.

After the plays the girls danced in the gymnasium. Dorothy Hambright read the prophecy.

Football Banquet

Twenty-eight of the 1922 football squad, faculty members and guests, were present at the annual Football Banquet given by the Decatur High School Athletic Association. Payton Helphinstine, center on the team during the seasons of '21 and '22 was elected to captain the 1923 squad. With eight letter-men returning and a wealth of material coming from the two Junior High Schools, Decatur High should look forward to a great year in football.

Talks centering on clean and wholesome living for a successful athlete were made by Rev. R. E. Henry, Principal T. M. Deam, Superintendent Richeson, H. M. Owen and Coach William G. Muir. A successful year was prophesied by all the speakers. The six men who graduate also made short talks.

Calendar

Sept. 3—Registration. Hello everybody!
Sept. 6—Ten minute periods. Now we're in 322! Everybody talks.
Sept. 7—We begin to work!

Sept. 13—Literary Societies have first meetings.
Sept. 15—Superintendent Richeson welcomes us back.
Sept. 20—Are we good? Oh my yes! Decatur walks off with the Grand Prize at State Fair.! Right in Springfield too!
Sept. 21—We liked Hawver but—Oh, Lester!
Sept. 22—Observer and Decanois staffs chosen (and they gave us this job!).
Sept. 25—Who is the football hero? Buy your ticket early and avoid the rush!
Sept. 26—Mad rush between Dorothy and Helen to win the prize Glenn or Tommy, which shall it be?
Sept. 28—We show off our prize winning exhibits to our fathers and mothers. Glenn and Tommy are still in the lead.

Sept. 29—Behold the most popular football player—Mr. Thomas O'Connell.
Sept. 30—One game and a good man lost! Kile gets his leg broken. Monticello 6—Decatur 0.

Oct. 2—The grave and reverend seniors meet for the first time.

Oct. 4—Glenn McClelland elected senior president.

Oct. 7—We beat the Jacksonville School for Deaf 7-0. Never say the band didn't help a lot!

Oct. 11-13—Teachers' Institute. Of course we hate to miss school but —you know how 'tis!

Oct. 14—Decatur 13—Mattoon 3. More banquets for the team!

Oct. 18—Admiral Moore tells us the whys and wherefores of the new Constitution.

Oct. 19—Juniors elect officers. Clare Sober president.

Oct. 21—Sad news! Decatur 0—Urbana 45!

Oct. 25—Now we know where all those classy popular songs come from! Mr. Louvaine told us! He also demonstrated on the piano! Wonder what opera suggested "Mr. Gallagher"!

Oct. 26—Athletic Association banquet for all "D" men. We wish we could play basketball or football or something.

Oct. 27—More sad news. Peoria 24—Decatur 9. Oh well, catastrophes will occur!

Nov. 1—James Rattan presents plan for Student Council to us in auditorium.

Nov. 4—As some of our football heroes were disabled the game with Bloomington was called off.

Nov. 6—We have with us Good English Week. Everyone windeth his tongue carefully.

Nov. 7—General election day. Did the Socialists win?

The Success of the

Decanois

depends on

The Advertisers

Support Them

These merchants represent
the best and most progress-
ive merchants in the city.
The Advertisers Helped Us
Let Us Help Them

Nov. 8—Although she is timid, shy and retiring, we finally persuaded Miss Jackson to speak in auditorium on the joys of football. Lotsa pep?

Nov. 11—In spite of Miss Jackson's speech we lose to Danville 13-3. Mud, mud and more mud! It's a good thing for the football boys that it was Saturday night so they could apply the Ivory! And the Juniors "threw" a party. A lovely time was had by all.

Nov. 14—Why doesn't somebody do something around this place to give us something to write about? Won't somebody jump into the roaring Sangamon, or fall down steps, or get married? We're not particular what they do?

Nov. 17—"The Think's the thing" according to the Senior Motto. "We can because we think we can." That's truly noble.

Nov. 19—The Agora and Aristos girls eat.

Nov. 24-26—What a blessed thing is Teachers' Institute! We should think they'd have them more often.

Nov. 27—After long absence, we once more behold Glenn's countenance. Did he bring Dorothy W. a Robert's Rule of Order for taking care of the Senior meetings for him? We hope so!

Nov. 28—Mask and Wig presents, "The Turtle Dove." Did we, or did we not hear Bill say to Vic "My little Orange Blossom, come to me."

Nov. 29—Mr. Holt and Mr. Irving speak in auditorium.

Nov. 30—We play with Springfield today. Score 21-3 for Springfield. What have we to be thankful for?

The
Millikin National Bank

Oldest—Largest Bank in Decatur

[Founded A. D., 1860]

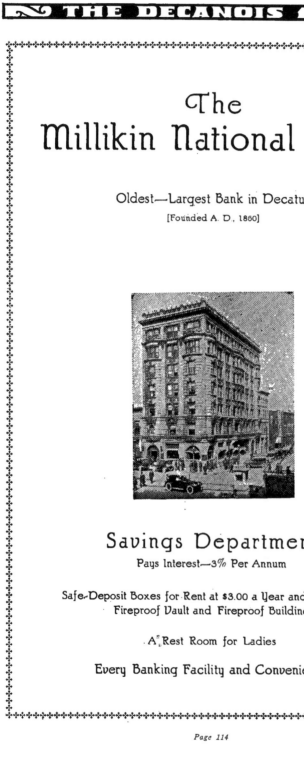

Savings Department

Pays Interest—3% Per Annum

Safe-Deposit Boxes for Rent at $3.00 a Year and Upward in
Fireproof Vault and Fireproof Building

A Rest Room for Ladies

Every Banking Facility and Convenience

Dec. 3—Bettie Holt, Marjorie Sullivan, Karl Kolkers, and Maurine Evans win first, second, third and fourth place in Review Story Contest.

Dec. 4—Miss Penrod sporteth a diamond. Much speculation occasioned by some.

Dec. 5—What won't those clever boys think of! Now we have toreador trousers!

Dec. 6—Tuscola 26—Decatur 13.

Dec. 12—Miss Trostle tells us about the poor children in the Near East.

Dec. 13—Booster meeting for our debaters—not that they need it.

Dec. 22—Christmas party in gym. Jack Eisele makes a wonderful Santa Claus!

Dec. 23—Forum-Rotaro Dance.

Dec. 23-Jan. 2—Christmas Vacation. How we hate to miss school!

Jan. 1—"Happy New Year."

Jan. 2—Back to the old grind! I wonder how long these good resolutions all about *A* reports will last!

Jan. 3—Auditorium for Mask and Wig play.

Jan. 4—Don't we wish we had a diamond ring like Miss Engle's?

Jan. 5—Decatur 21—Monticello 23.. A mere detail of course. Also "The Man Who Married a Dumb Wife." And was she dumb!!!

Jan. 6—More mere details, Tuscola 16—Decatur 13.

Jan. 8—Have you pledged your "Dek" yet? Watch the barometer rise.

Jan. 9—And still it rises.

Jan. 10—Mrs. Tommasi sings in auditorium.

Jan. 12—Picture taken in auditorium.

Jan. 13—Urbana—Decatur.

Jan. 18—Mr. Kenney speaks on "Thrifts."

Jan. 19—This is almost too sad to write. Springfield 29—Decatur 11.

Jan. 24—Exams.

Jan. 25—More Exams!!

Jan. 26—G. A. A. Dance. My, but those girl athletes are a noisy, rowdy bunch! Girls, I am afraid that you can't have any more parties unless you mend your ways.

Jan. 27—Run up the flag! Call out the band. We have won a game!!! Decatur 29—Maroa 25.

Jan. 28—Marjorie Sullivan goes to Chicago. Don't let anything get you in the big city, Marge.

Jan. 29—Kippy, the Frisco King, and Coffey, the Frisco Queen! Some couple!

Jan. 31—Senior Play tryout. Wonder where all the would-be actors and actresses came from.

Feb. 1—Ten minute schedules for the second semester.

Feb. 9—A special to Springfield!! Lots of fun, but oh, my! Decatur 12, Springfield 28.

Feb. 10—Anyhow we beat Monticello!

Feb. 12—Dr. Davis speaks in auditorium.

Feb. 14—"Will you be my Valentine?"

Feb. 17—Eleanor and Boliver have a slight disagreement.
    And right so soon after Valentine's Day.
    Oh well in the course of time true love never runs smooth.

Feb. 22—Washington's birthday. Auditorium to show our appreciation of our forefather.

Feb. 24—Grand rush to Wasson's.

Feb. 26—Fire! Fire! Only a false alarm.

Mar. 1—Come in like a lamb, but oh my! how it will go out.

Mar. 2, 3, 4—Tournament. Decatur places third.

Wisdom in Few Words
— *Only Doing Counts*

BENJAMIN FRANKLIN'S wisdom had many sides, but it shone brightest in the homely, kindly and quaint advice he gave to people, young and old, rich and poor, about how to live their lives.

Not what you profess is important, nor what you think, he believed. But it is what you do that counts.

He did not expect everybody to take his advice but many people in many lands have learned how to become, *"healthy, wealthy, and wise"* since *Franklin's* time by a study of his proverbs.

The National Bank *of* Decatur

"Decatur's Oldest National Bank"

Mar. 4—Hats off to Miss Sprunger. Congratulations Asa.

Mar. 5—Mr. Miller's engagement announced.

Mar. 9—Sectional Tournament. Villa Grove wins.

Mar. 14—Auditorium—Girl's Glee Club.

       Music hath charms—and we're all charmed.

Mar. 17—Spring fever makes its first appearance. Chink and Lucille think they'll go swimming. "Hang your clothes on a hickory limb but don't go near the water!"

Mar. 19—Sophomores beat Juniors.

Mar. 22—Sophomores beat Seniors. Rah!! Rah!!

Mar. 23—Quite a busy day.

       Senior Play—"Such A Little Queen."

       "Farewell, Miss Engle. Congratulations."

       Spring Vacation starts.

       Now you can go swimming Chink.

Apr. 1—April Fool! But oh my! It was Sunday and lots of new clothes were seen.

Apr. 3—Hard to work after a week's rest. It must be done.

Apr. 4—"90 pounds of hairpins and paint until two in the morning"— Tommy Ryan.

Apr. 5—We shall now proceed to propound this time honored riddle— "That grass reminds me of Freshmen." "Why?" "Oh, it's so green!" Clever?

Apr. 10—Senior Class meeting.

Apr. 11—Mr. Hubbart wonders why the girls are always dropping their complexions! We'll bite, why are they? But we hope that Mr. Hubbart will not lose any sleep trying to solve it.

Apr. 12—Miss Ruby Engle changes her last name. Oh! yes, it took place in Chicago.

Apr. 13—Senior pictures much in evidence. Speak up girls!! Rattan has lots.

Apr. 16—We begin to look for that $1.50 for a Decanois.

Apr. 18—Miss Neilson speaks to us in auditorium and then gives a few of us a special treat in 110. Behold! Edna Espy, our rising your actress. "Oh see the beautiful rose."

Apr. 20—One of those dances under the personal supervision of Miss Winnifred Wilson.

Apr. 23—Spring fever is much in evidence. Even Bohon failed to recite in English.

Apr. 24—Glenn McClelland chosen as Valedictorian.

Apr. 27—James Rattan is picked as Salutatorian.

Apr. 28—Junior-Senior Reception. We thank you very much, Juniors, for the wonderful party.

May 1—May Day.   Oh! why didn't we get out of school?

May 7—We wonder if this is blue Monday.   Ask Miss Hull.

May 10—Miss Bridges just about empties 322 this morning with her announcement: "May I see the following in 320 before the first hour?"

May 11—Rotaro-Forum Banquet and they invited their lady friends.

May 14—Spring fever is again peeping up here and there.

May 18—Chester Napoleon Walker in "Swords and Scissors."
        Where's Josephine, Chet?

May 26—Agora and Aristos eat again at their picnic.   My how these girls can eat.   I wonder how the fellows will ever be able to support them.

June 1—Senior Class Day—
        Auditorium and honors are awarded.
        Then the real picnic!

June 4-5—Our last exams in D. H. S.   Such grades!

June 8—Commencement and it wound up with a dance in the evening. Were we happy?   I'll say we were!

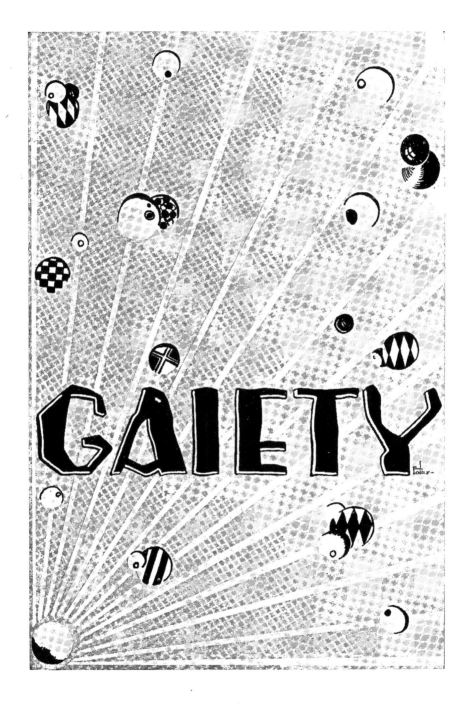

WILLIAM GUSHARD CO.

Confidence

BEFORE the golden age of Greece, before the Empire of Egypt, before ancient China existed, Phoenicia thrived. Thirty-six centuries she endured; a longer supremacy than may be credited to any other. nation. Her strength came from world commerce; her endurance from world confidence.

In this store we realize the importance of public confidence. It is our most precious possession; our most valuable asset; the highest reward of the patrons we have served. To safeguard and inspire confidence is our most important duty.

For that reason we strive to serve carefully and cheerfully; to consistently bring to our patrons merchandise of the finest possible quality at the lowest possible price; to adhere strictly to truth in advertising and selling; to deal courteously with everyone who passes through our doors; to offer the fullest measure of efficient service to each of our patrons; and to guarantee satisfaction to every purchaser.

These are the policies we have adhered to for many years, until at last their practice has become a habit. They are policies followed without effort, for their observance has become a matter of course.

They are builders of public confidence, and confidence is the guide to success in business and life.

DECATUR'S GREATEST STORE

FAMILIAR SAYINGS BY FAMILIAR PEOPLE

"Go to the office." ....Miss Griffin
"Say! Listen!" ....William G. Muir
"Think so?" ....Miss Kinsey
"See my diamond?" ....Miss Penrod
"Lynn, keep still." ....Miss Ormsby
"Who's the fifth person at this table?" ....Mr. Radcliffe
"We will have a test tomorrow." ....Miss Hill
"Yea! Decatur!" ....Miss Hull
"May I see you in Room 320 before the first hour?".........Miss Bridges
"The seats in this room are better than those at Columbia University"...
....Miss Fritter
"As I tell my Sociology Class." ....Mr. Deam
"Those whom I have marked absent in this section are —".....Miss English
"You don't know, do you?" ....Wiz Tait
"How now, good my friend." ....Bill Pitner
"This demonstration will be given both evening and night."...........
....Rassele Swarthout
"You know my gospel, young people." ....Mrs. Nelson
"The 18th lesson is due tomorrow." ....Miss N. Engle
"I want to see you back here the 8th hour." ....Miss Whitcraft
"Glenn McClelland will read the announcements." ....Miss English
"Mein Gott!" ....Mr. Tommasi
"Are you late?" ....Mr. Sprunger
"I wouldn't bluff." ....Mr. Nordman
"I can't admit you." ....Mrs. Hostetler

WHICH IS WORSE?

This remark was made in an American history class. "The coming of William Pitner into office in England caused the English to win in the struggle against France. This remark was also made in the same class "Molasses was raised in the West Indies, oh! I mean cane was raised."

V. Elliott—"What did you say?"
B. Whittle—"Nothing."
"Vick"—"I know that, but I wondered how you expressed it this time."

E. Logan (with much enthusiasm)—"I could go on dancing like this with you forever."
D. Abaly—"Oh, no, you couldn't possibly. You're bound to improve."

Vistor (to Herman P.)—"Is the effective speaking teacher a good one?"
Herman—"I'll say she is, she's a Bear."

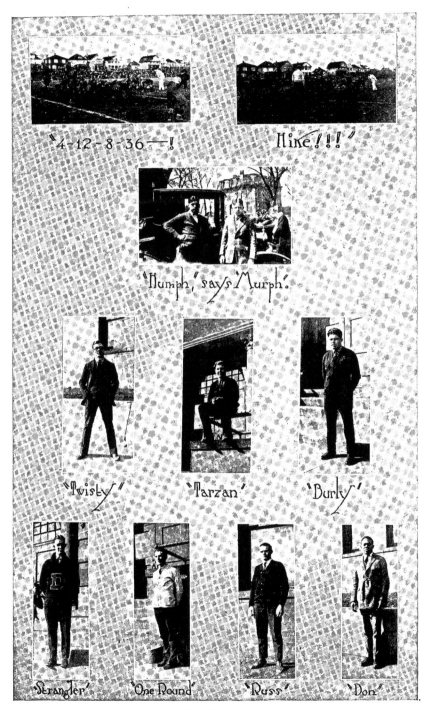

"4-12-8-36—!"   "Hike!!!"

"Humph," says "Murph".

"Twisty"   "Tarzan"   "Burly"

"Strangler"   "One Round"   "Russ"   "Don"

After You Graduate
WHAT SCHOOL?

Who's Who in Decatur High School

The Cheer Leader ....Lester Foltz
The Shiek ....Wallace Hogle
The He-Flapper ....Merril DeBaum
The Man ....James Rattan
The Flirt ....Dorothy Abaly
Married Life ....Dorothy Mae and Tom
Fashion Plate ....Walter Johnson
The Bachelor ....Bernard Royer
The Frisco ....Elizabeth Tait
The Divorcee ....Tom Riggs
The Flapper ....Martha Holt
The Artist ....Helen Hackett
The King ....Glenn McClelland
The Queen ....Bonnie Regan
The Cave Man ....William Williams
The Clown ....Jane Pluck
The Ladies' Man ....Lealdes Eaton
The Home Breaker ....Catherine Coffey
The Athlete ....Paul Offenstein
The Lady of Fashion ....Iva Brennen
Gold Dust Twins ....
......Doris Kelly and Catherine Graham
The Senior ....Louise Mason
Baby Talk Ladies ....
.......Birdie Webb and Lucile Ehrhart
The Ancient Mariner ....Carl Jenkins

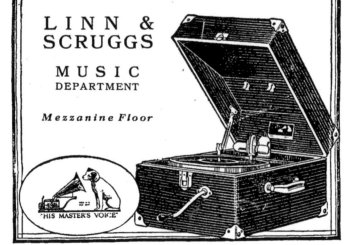

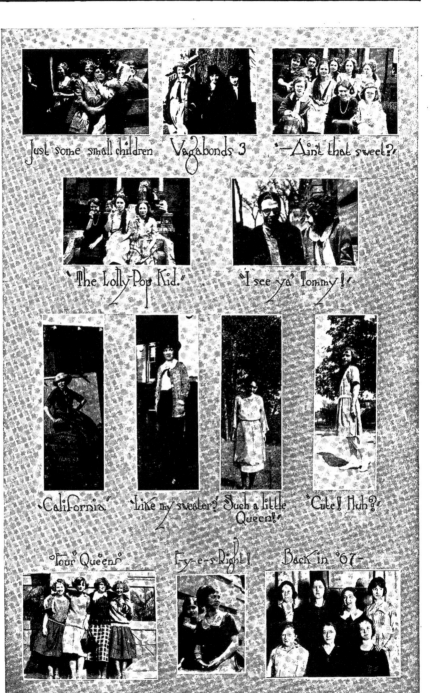

Just some small children   Vagabonds 3   "—Ain't that sweet?"

"The Lolly-Pop Kid."   "I see ya' Tommy!"

"California"   "Like my sweater?" "Such a little
Queen!"   "Cute! Huh?"

"Four Queens"   Ey-e-s Right!   Back in '67—

A LETTER

Dear Dottie Mae—

Honestly I'm awfully sorry for the way I acted last night. I do not know now what I was mad at. But I do want you to forgive me. It made me feel terrible because you acted so sweet when I was that way. You never said a cross word. It's your sweetness that gets me. When I'm peeved you are always so sweet.

Please forgive me this once. I wrote this just as soon as I got home from your house so I could give it to you in the morning. Answer.

As Ever Yours,

Tom.

Oakey—"Dee Gee wouldn't go with you."
Boliver—"No, but Eleanor Wood."

Mrs. Eaton—"How is is that you spend your allowance so fast?"
Lee—"I'm helping out these poor Eskimos by buying their pies."

I'M HUNGRY CLUB

President ....Crawford Francis
Vice-President ....Wm. Robinson
Treasurer ....Francis Harrold
Secretary ....Paul Offenstein
Time of Meeting—At the end of 3rd hour everyday.
Place—High school Hamburger Counter.

Mr. Deams' Favorite Students——?

George Maxon   Lynn Pensinger
Les Foltz   Virgil Bailey
Wallace Hogle   Thomas Riggs

"WONDER WHYS" OF 322

Wonder why James Rattan falls heir to the reading of the Bulletin when the president is absent.

Wonder why Rassele Swarthout has such a glib tongue after the ringing of the bell.

Wonder why the President of the Senior Class should have business with the Vice-President (Dot Wilson) during Home Room period.

Wonder why there were so many conferences with the Senior Advisors the day after the first six weeks grades were given out.

Rattan Tire Company

Wholesale and Retail

Telephone Main 873

256 North Park Street

Decatur, Illinois

Looking for fish — Pullets — Sailing Sailing

Oh!! — Hold your head up — Prof. Tomato — Sizzle!!☆! — Yours?

Grin! Dern ye! — A bunch of bums — The one and only.

N. by N. E. on Lake Decatur — Beans!

TRASH

The Grassville Times
Grassville's Greatest Newspaper

Napkin
Final
Edition

PUBLISHED once a year, whether you get more than one copy or not.

PRICE—$0.00 per week. Same price weekly. Absolutely no free subs.

EDITORIAL POLICY—The why and when of the Asparagus Leaf—Why it cuts baby's teeth, and its effect on suspenders on a winter day.

WE SPONSOR—The Wreck of the Hesperus and the Easter Rabbit.

OUR MORAL IS—"Quin hic oppidorum dumbis."

WARNING—Please don't sue us for libel—It might hurt our feelings.

THIS ISSUE DEDICATED—To the Last Rose of Summer, at Custer's last Stand, on the night that Trotzky was killed for the 53rd time.

HIGH SCHOOL BOY SUICIDE

SENIOR CLASS PRESIDENT LAYS IN TWO YEAR SUPPLY

The Woolworth Store reported today that Glenn McClelland bought 50 pairs of the best grade of socks and said he was going to lay in a two years supply. This shows very good judgment on the part of Mr. McClelland, and we hope some others will follow his example. The socks are 10c apiece, but are sold only by the pair.

MAYOR LEAVES FOR ANTIOCH

Our Mayor, Mr. Lealdes Eaton, left early today for Antioch, to visit his great, great grandfather, who is on his death bed. Mr. Eaton ordered flowers before he left.

Latest reports say Mr. Eaton's relative died before he arrived so the order for flowers was cancelled.

Buy Sure-Kure for colds and toothache.

NEW MOVIE HOUSE OPENS

The Hippodrome, a new, modern movie house, has opened up here lately.

A special organ attachment with the local boiler works, and the city hall gives the music.

A new film will be shown tomorrow, "The Lights of Broadway"; a thrilling tale of the Northwest, starring Dynamite Pritchett and Moonbeam Pollock. The Pathe News of Armistice Day will be shown also.

SHERIFF TO HOLD ELECTION

Sheriff Swarthout announced today that he would hold a public election, as to whether he should continue as sheriff or devote his life to the stage.

Everette Witzeman Takes Gas After Being Refused in Proposal

Mr. E. Witzeman, a student of the D. H. S. committed suicide early this morning by taking gas. His folks are worried about the bill, for the gas was left on, he having forgotten to turn it off after getting enough. It is thought that his sweetheart, Nancy Hill, turned him down when he proposed to her.

MYSTERY SOLVED

W. Pitner Still With Us

"Little Willy" Pitner thought missing, was found today by Detective Kretzinger. Pitner's mother received a box yesterday marked "Bill Inside," and promptly fainted. Kretzinger, who is a graduate of the Veville Katchum School, opened the supposed coffin and found it contained only Mr. Pitner's salary as commissioner. The "bill" was from Linxweiler and Hornback, printers.

LOCAL PAGE

NEW COMPANY TO BUILD HERE

GRASSVILLE IS AGAIN FORTUNATE

The Grassville Times, Grassville's Greatest Newspaper, is pleased to announce that Mr. T. Bohon, President of the Auto-Mat Pancake Flopper company, in a special correspondence to the Grassville Times, Grassville's Greatest Newspaper, states that his company will build a $300,000 plant here next month. He says that this is only a branch factory. The company is a good one, so Mr. Bohon says, and manufactures Automatic Pancake Floppers which retail at the Piggly Wiggly stores at 98c and at Woolworth's for 10c.

Mr. Bohon says: "We know we will like Grassville because of the public-spirited officials and fine citizens Grassville produces."

Mr. Bohon also complimented the Grassville Times, Grassville's Greatest Newspaper. He said: "I read a copy of the Grassville Times, Grassville's Greatest Newspaper, and enjoyed it very much. It burns better than most papers."

Mr. Eaton, our mayor, was out of town when Mr. Bohon arrived, but will meet him when the company comes to start the construction of their plant.

PET DOG DIES AS RESULT OF INJURIES

Miss Dorothy Wilson, daughter of Mr. and Mrs. H. F. Wilson, regular patrons of the Grassville Times, Grassville's Greatest Newspaper, bemoans the loss of her poodle dog, which was killed by the noon Express at 4:50 P. M. Sunday morning.

PRISONER ESCAPES FROM COUNTY JAIL

Just as Sheriff Swarthout was feeding his horse in the stable, Joe Rosenberg, famous combination twidler, called for help in his cell. Sheriff Swarthout ran to see what was the matter, and was knocked senseless by a piece of cake, Mr. Rosenberg's missile. The prisoner then escaped. His whereabouts are unknown, but Niantic, Boody and Decatur are looking for him.

Four suspects have been arrested at Harristown, while Faries Park boasts six. Federal Officer Harrold is on the way to assist in the search.

Public Notices

Mr. William B. V. D. Pitner will address the Hopeless Club in the club rooms at 2:30 P. M. at 4 o'clock tomorrow night. The subject will be "A silo is round for the same reason that a hairless head is bald".

Professor Nathan Haines will give a lecture at the Decatur High School entitled "Miscellaneous Perplexities of Egyptian Dancing". Admission 50c. Time—7:30 Tonight. Come! Come!

Mr. Theodore Brown will lecture on "Complaint Complexities Concerning Correlative Concoctions," after the Haines Lecture, if the audience survives—"Bring the Kiddies."

Macon County Coal Company

Riverside Sootless
Domestic Lump

Coal

Telephones: Main 77 and 78

FOREST FILE, *General Manager*

THE GRASSVILLE TIMES—Grassville's Greatest Newspaper

SOCIETY PAGE
FARM NEWS

SOCIETY PAGE

NEW PLOW INVENTED

ERICK WINTERS JOINS "400"

Has Attained Long Hoped For Social Prominence

Mr. Erick Winters has at last attained the ambition of his life. He has been admitted to the "400" society group of New York. His debump was at Astor's Ball at the Blue Ribbon, last Friday evening. Mr. Winters was formerly employed at the Decatur Herald, The Grassville Times, Grassville's Greatest Newspaper's only beaten rival. Mr. Winters is now employed as head waiter at the Blue Ribbon.

Mr. and Mrs. Junior (Pete) Rothfuss left on their annual roundup trip to Alaska early this morning. They left very unexpectedly, as Sheriff Swarthout didn't give them much time. Mrs Rothfuss was formerly Helen Willard.

ECKERT BUYS "SPARKIE"

Famous Horse Now in Hands of Local Fan

Mr. Mathias Eckert has just returned from Podunk where he purchased the famous race horse "Sparkplug" from its former owner.

Mr. Eckert says that outside of one game leg and a glass eye the horse is in the pink of condition.

LIVELY TIME IN CIRCUIT COURT

Judge Danzeisen Refuses to Lower Dignity

When Judge Danzeisen opened court yesterday morning at 2:30 P. M. he found a divorce case awaiting him. One of the important witnesses was absent, so the judge was asked to take his place But when the lawyer had to hit the witness with a rolling pin to show how much damage was done the judge ruled it out of order.

However, when the wife who was supposedly mistreated, and who was formerly Miss Betty Holt testified against C. Sober the divorce was readily granted. The judge then adjourned court to eat dinner at the Liberty.

Willard Hansen Says Invention Will Mean a Fortune

Mr. Willard Hansen, graduate of the Grassville High School, invented an occulating, revolving, self-condescending, transferable, take-down-able, and evolutionary plow by accident last week, and has it perfected for manufacturing. He says it should bring him a fortune. He has found 56 improvements over the old kind. He intends to find one more and become a rival of Heinz.

LADY AUCTIONEER

Miss Zola Sloan announced late yesterday, that, contrary to previous reports, she would become the first recorded lady auctioneer. Miss Sloan has had experience in hypnotism while debating on the D. H. S. team. We wish her luck, but hope the listeners don't suffocate.

To the Public

I openly announce my candidacy for Mayor of Grassville. I appeal to the peaceful, law-abiding, lovely, magnificient, and fumigated citizens of Grassville for their support in the election some Tuesday next week.

I am recommended by Sing-Sing and Trotsky.

Yours till Niagra Falls,

JAMES RATTAN

Here —
and

There.

SONGOLOGY

Baby Blue Eyes ....Helen Johns
Dumbell ....Most of Us
All Muddled Up ....Edna Espy
Homesick ....Hal Williams
I'm Just Wild about Harry ....Emily Johnson
Kitten on the Keys ....Lois Boyd (Meow)
Jimmy ....Lonnie Banta
Lovin' Sam ....Marcellus Pope
St, Louis Blues ....Wally Johnson
The Sneak ....Neva Neal
The Flapper Walk ....Edith Chapman
My Little Margie ....Jack Lanum
The Waltz Is Made for Love ....Clare and Bettie
Struttin' Blues ....Kippy Pensinger
Take Your Girlie to the Movies if You Can't Make Love at Home .....
....Bill and Vivian
Aggravatin' Papa ....Mr. Deam
I'm So Glad My Mammy Don't Know Where I'm At ......The Holt Sisters
Chicago ....Marge Sullivan

Mr. Hubbart (in Economics)—"What is the seller's (cellar) Surplus?"
John McDonald—"I don't know, Pop hasn't been able to get any."

"Ever study a blotter?"
"No, foolish."
"Very absorbing thing."

Dorothy Boyer in the sixth hour class translating Spanish:
The cowboy lassoed the horse and the latter burst out laughing.

Mrs. Nelson (reviewing essays)—"Glenn you took the *Saturday Night Bath,* did you not?"
Mac—"Yes'm, I did."

In 7th hour Industrial Drawing class Art Jackson was leaning on two legs of his chair. The chair slipped and fell. Mr. Rotz said—"Art sit on four legs."

Wonder what will happen to Miss Crea next fall?

Go on and
whistle

Showing the age
range in our school?

'Vanna
bite?'

Mighty happy

Joseph Dehrns Nordman!

'Sixty'

'Emo' and Bolver'

Whoa!! Sparky!

'Mac'

for

Vacation Days—

Tennis Supplies	Guns
Golf Equipment	Ammunition
Base Ball Goods	Thermos Bottle
Bathing Suits	Athletic Clothing
Fishing Tackle	Athletic Shoes
Canoes	Camp Equipment
Row Boats	Tourist Supplies
Boat Motors	Hammocks

Sporting Goods Department

Morehouse & Wells Company

"The Best Grade for the Best Trade"

BASKET BALL

"Bush"　　"Big Boy"　　"Mitch"　　"Twisty"

"Six Seconds" McGowan
and
His Crew.

"Tuffy"　　　　　Same as above

"Jim"　　"Surefire"　　D.C.'s Best　　Cap'n John

A HOME RUN

A jingle, a scuffle,
The second bells rung,
A hubbub of voices
Intermission's begun.

Now run to your locker
Grab one book or more,
A mirror and powder
Now slam the door.

Make use of your mirror,
"Are my lips on straight?"
But hurry a bit faster
You're almost late.

A rush down the stairway
A breathless home run
At last your safe for
The bell has just rung.

OH—HOW—SHE—CAN—DANCE

Perhaps she couldn't bake a cake,
Or broil for me my evening steak;
I doubt if she would deign to think
Of working at a kitchen sink,
But—Oh—man—how—she—dances.

I know she couldn't fix a chair,
Or press a suit or mend a tear;
I doubt if she can play or sing,
Or do a single useful thing;
But—oh—man—how—she—dances.

She probably isn't very bright,
In class—but take her out at night,
I'm sure you'll find that she'll all right;
For—oh—boy—how—she—dances.

ENGLISH VI

English isn't hard
    'Till you get as far as VI,
And then it seems to me
    That my brain just sticks.

I can't make things rhyme
    And that's what you have to do
So I think I'll go again
    Back to good old English II.

Hal Williams—(as expressed by *himself!*)
    I am the sheik—
    All the girls are unable to resist me—
    I have a "pull" with the teachers—
    I get over "big" with everyone—
    I can date any girl in town—
        Because look who I am!

My girl's not much
    She doesn't know
What makes the seasons
    Come and go.

She couldn't name
    The farthest star
Or tell you what
    Electrons are.

But say! I'll tell
    The whole world wide,
She knows her stuff—
    I'm satisfied.

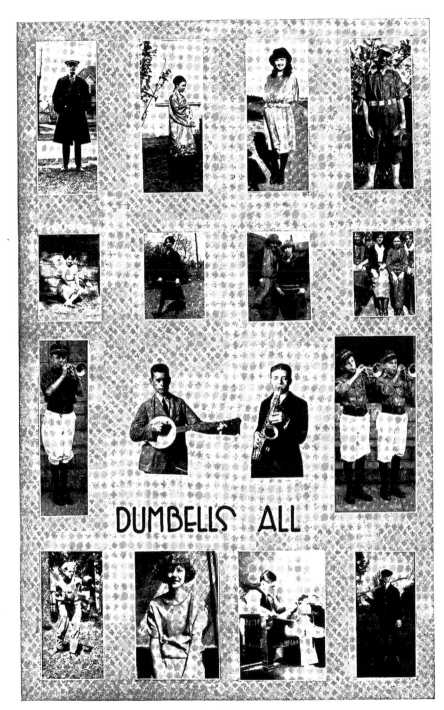

DUMBELLS ALL

RADIO NEWS

Rassele got a new station the other night. He stuck his head out the window and got Chile.

"A palmist", wrote a youngster, "is a woman who uses her hand instead of a slipper."

"The difference between an elephant and a microbe," wrote another, "is that one carries a trunk, and the other carries the grip."

Senior—"How did you come out in that exam?"
Junior—"Oh, I knocked it for a loop."
Senior—"Howzat? A hundred?"
Junior—"No, a zero."

WRIGLEY CHEWING SOCIETY

OUR AIM: To abolish all gum chewing within the building of the Decatur High School.

We have previously tried to set examples to our fellow students.
Lord High Endurance .... Martha Holt
Presidential Popper .... Edith Chapman
Secretarial Cracker .... Virginia Dawson
Gimme Some, Advisor .... Dorothy Abaly
Meetings are held daily.

> There was a small youth and his mother,
> Went to see his mother's young brother,
> But they had the same name,
> And they looked just the same,
> So the mother couldn't tell one from the other.

"What are you doing up there, building a bird house?"
"No, foolish; I'm erecting a service station for flying-fish."

Mr. Westlund—"Why didn't you filter this?"
Joe Rosenberg—"I didn't think it would stand the strain."

Every year in every way I get a credit here and a credit there.—Bob Logan.

The James Millikin University

Decatur College of Millikin University is classed as A-1 by all standardizing agencies.

Many Decatur High School "Grads" realize that Millikin University is one of the important factors that make Decatur "The Biggest Little City on Earth."

Many also realize that they can "buy in Decatur", secure a college education at home and save money in so doing.

Here at home they may enjoy the advantages of the best small college without the disadvantages of the large university.

Courses are offered in Liberal Arts, Engineering, Household Arts, Commerce and Finance, Fine and Applied Arts, Education, Music, Library Science, Biblical, Literature, Manual Training, Physical Training, etc. The advantages of their articulation in a compactly organized and well equipped institution of learning are readily seen by all who are conversant with modern educational progress.

The University authorities appreciate the patronage of students from Decatur High School and hope to welcome a good proportion of the class of 1923 in September.

For further details send for a catalog or call at the office.

"Tippy" and "Jinks"   "Katy" and Doris   "Newlie" and "Bert"

"Aw! Gee!!"   Betty   Ya-Yes!   G-r-r-r-!

2 Queens + a Jack   Skippin' Class   Yer' Pinched

Mr. Westlund telling of patent leather in seventh hour chemistry class.

Mr. Westlund—"Castor oil is put in patent leather so it will not be brittle and crack."

Linn H.—"What makes it crack then in the winter?"

James V.—"The castor oil freezes."

A flivver stood on the railroad track,
Its heart went plinkity-plunk,
The 2:49 came down the track,
TOOT—TOOT—Max Atlass.

Says the Compact:
The last link is broken
That bound me to thee,
And the fall thou hast allowed
Has render'd me free.

Wm. Pitner—"Why is real estate business so profitable?"

Alan Chapman (rather dumb as usual)—"Ask some one who knows."

W. P.—"Because there are always lots for sale."

If Clare's Sober, why isn't Goldie Jolly, and why doesn't Bill Whittle and Maurice Munch.

LAUGH AND THE WORLD LAUGHS WITH YOU
WEEP AND YOU WEEP ALONE

GOODBYE FOREVER

We Have a Line

of

Electric	Grills
Percolators	Mazda Lamps
Heating Pads	Fans and
Curling Irons	Gas Stoves
Disc Stoves	Waffle Irons
Electric Irons	Gas Heaters
Toasters	Gas Irons
Vibrators	Gas Mantles

[We are at your service and
will appreciate your patronage]

Decatur
Railway and Light Company

HIGH SCHOOL ANNUAL ENGRAVERS

Zinc Etchings
Copper Halftones
Art Work

CAPITOL ENGRAVING CO.
Post Office Court
Springfield
Ill.

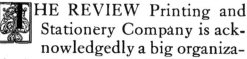